Kitchen Kaleidoscope

Dishcloths Collection

By Knit Picks

Photography by John Cranford

Printed in the United States of America

First Printing, 2020

ISBN 978-1-62767-261-0

Versa Press, Inc.
800-447-7829

www.versapress.com

A few notes for all patterns

Matching the exact recommended gauge is not critical for any dishcloth, but gauge does affect the size and the amount of yarn needed, so don't get too far off!

All sizes given are somewhat approximate.

Always choose a needle size to obtain gauge, which may be different from the recommended needle size (keeping in mind above notes about not worrying too much about gauge!).

How you choose to "block" your dishcloths is up to you; if you'll be using it to wash dishes, you may not see a point in washing it and laying it flat to block nicely. However, if you're giving it as a gift, you'll probably want to give it a quick wash and let it dry flat and smooth.

When gauge is listed as blocked, it generally doesn't mean pinned out, just washed and then dried flat, unless the pattern explains otherwise.

Read all flat chart RS rows (odd numbers) from right to left, and WS rows (even numbers) from left to right. (All charts are worked flat unless otherwise noted.)

DIAMOND LACE
by Jenny Williams

This pretty dishcloth will add a bit of elegance to your kitchen cleanup! Diamond motifs are created with simple yarn overs and decreases, framed by a Garter Stitch border.

FINISHED MEASUREMENTS
9.25″ × 9.25″

YARN
Dishie™ (worsted weight, 100% Cotton; 190 yards/100g); Clarity 27037, 1 skein

NEEDLES
US 5 (3.75mm) circular or straight needles

NOTIONS
Yarn Needle

GAUGE
19 sts and 30 rows = 4″ in Diamond Lace Chart, blocked

DIRECTIONS
CO 46 sts.

Row 1 (RS): Work Diamond Lace Chart (next page) Row 1. Cont in established pattern through Diamond Lace Chart Row 74.

BO all sts.

Finishing
Weave in the ends. Wash and block if desired.

Diamond Lace Chart

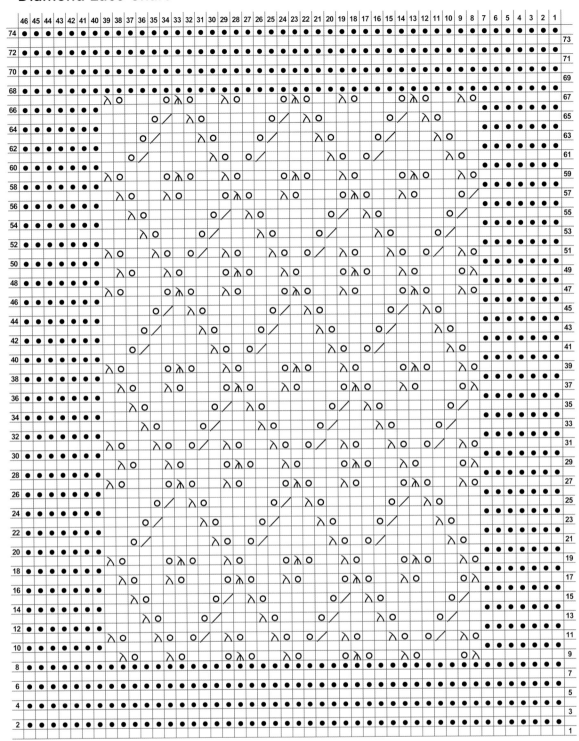

LEGEND

	K		K2tog
☐	RS: Knit stitch WS: Purl stitch	◢	Knit 2 stitches together as one stitch

	P		SKP
⊡	RS: Purl stitch WS: Knit stitch	⋌	Slip 1 knit-wise, knit 1, pass slip stitch over knit stitch

	YO		SK2P
⊙	Yarn over	⋏	Slip 1 knit-wise, K2tog, pass slip stitch over K2tog

SWITCHBACKS
by Violet LeBeaux

Switchbacks is a fun take on the traditional dishcloth. It uses a very simple mesh pattern leaning in different directions to create the zigzag effect. The stitches are easy to memorize so it makes for a great travel project.

FINISHED MEASUREMENTS
7" width × 6.75" height

YARN
Dishie™ (worsted weight, 100% Cotton; 190 yards/100g): Swan 25409, 1 skein

NEEDLES
US 6 (4mm) straight or circular needles

NOTIONS
Yarn Needle

GAUGE
18 sts and 24 rows = 4" in Switchbacks Mesh Pattern, blocked (note that these sections are very stretchy so gauge is approximate)

DIRECTIONS
Loosely CO 32 sts.
Row 1 (WS): P across.

Row 2 (RS): K1, (YO, K2tog) to last 1 st, K1.
Row 3: P1, (P2tog, YO) to last 1 st, P1.
Rep Rows 2–3 four more times.

Row 12: K1, (SSK, YO) to last 1 st, K1.
Row 13: P1, (YO, SSP) to last 1 st, P1.
Rep Rows 12–13 four more times.

Rep Rows 2–3 five times.
Rep Rows 12–13 five times.

Next Row: K across.
BO all sts.

Finishing
Weave in ends, wash, and block to measurements.

BASEBALL
by Emily Ringelman

Play ball! This washcloth will be a home run for any baseball fanatic. Knit in a single color, the baseball "laces" are created with embroidery. Fun and quick, you'll be able to make one for every Little Leaguer you know in no time at all.

This washcloth is worked from the bottom up with simple shaping and a Garter Stitch edge to prevent rolling. Stitches are added in the contrasting color at the end.

FINISHED MEASUREMENTS
7" across

YARN
Dishie™ (worsted weight, 100% Cotton; 190 yards/100g): MC Swan 25409, CC Fiesta Red 25786, 1 skein each

NEEDLES
US 7 (4.5m) straight or circular needles

NOTIONS
Yarn Needle
Stitch Markers

GAUGE
20 sts and 28 rows = 4" in Stockinette Stitch worked flat, blocked

DIRECTIONS
With MC, CO 8 sts.
Row 1 (WS): KFB, K6, KFB. 2 sts inc.
Row 2 (RS): KFB, K8, KFB. 2 sts inc.
Row 3: KFB, K10, KFB. 2 sts inc.
Row 4: KFB, K to last 2 sts, KFB, K1. 2 sts inc.
Row 5: K1, KFB, P to last 2 sts, K1, KFB. 2 sts inc.
Rep the last two rows once more. 22 sts.

Row 8: KFB, K to 2 sts from end, KFB, K1. 2 sts inc.
Row 9: K3, P to last 3 sts, K3.
Rep the last two rows six more times. 36 sts.

Row 22: K across.
Row 23: K3, P to last 3 sts, K3.
Rep the last two rows six more times.

Row 36: SSK, K to last 2 sts, K2tog. 2 sts dec.
Row 37: K3, P to last 3 sts, K3.
Rep the last two rows five more times. 24 sts.

Row 48: SSK, K to last 2 sts, K2tog. 2 sts dec.
Row 49: SSK, K1, P to last 3 sts, K1, K2tog. 2 sts dec.
Rep the last two rows three times. 8 sts.

BO K-wise.

Finishing
Weave in ends, wash, and block to diagram.

Cut a length of CC. Working from Duplicate Stitch Chart or copying the sample piece, embroider laces onto the baseball, using a running stitch. Weave in remaining ends.

Duplicate Stitch Chart

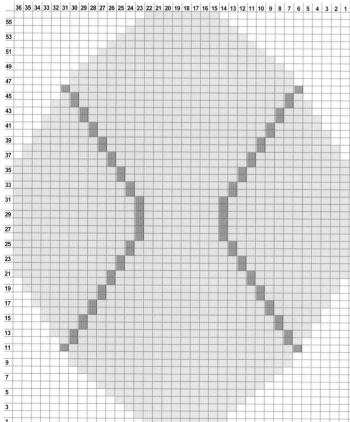

LEGEND

☐ Main Color

▨ Duplicate Stitch with Contrasting Color

GARDEN WINDOW
by Violet LeBeaux

Garden Window is a simple dishcloth featuring a mock eyelet cable up each side like vines climbing around a window. It has a Garter Stitch border and a Stockinette Stitch interior. The easy 4-row repeat creating the eyelet columns is a great way for a beginner to try something a little interesting.

FINISHED MEASUREMENTS
7.25″ width × 7.5″ height

YARN
Dishie™ (worsted weight, 100% Cotton; 190 yards/100g): Swan 25409, 1 skein

NEEDLES
US 6 (4mm) straight or circular needles

NOTIONS
Yarn Needle

GAUGE
18 sts and 24 rows = 4″ in Stockinette Stitch, blocked
18 sts and 40 rows = 4″ in Garter Stitch, blocked

Eyelet Pattern (flat over 7 sts)
Row 1 (RS): K1, P1, Sl1, K2, PSSO, P1, K1.
Row 2 (WS): P1, K1, P1, YO, P1, K1, P1.
Row 3: K1, P1, K3, P1, K1.
Row 4: P1, K1, P3, K1, P1.
Rep Rows 1–4 for pattern.

DIRECTIONS
Loosely CO 32 sts.
Rows 1–6: K across.

Row 7: K3, work Eyelet Pattern Row 1, K to last 10 sts, work Eyelet Pattern Row 1, K3.
Row 8: K3, work Eyelet Pattern Row 2, P to last 9 sts, work Eyelet Pattern Row 2, K3.
Row 9: K3, work Eyelet Pattern Row 3, K to last 10 sts, work Eyelet Pattern Row 3, K3.
Row 10: K3, work Eyelet Pattern Row 4, P to last 10 sts, work Eyelet Pattern Row 4, K3.
Rep Rows 7–10 until desired length is reached, ending on Row 2 of Eyelet Pattern.

Next 6 Rows: K across.
BO all sts.

Finishing
Weave in ends, wash, and block to measurements.

Eyelet Pattern

	7	6	5	4	3	2	1
4		●				●	
		●				●	3
2		●		O		●	
		●				●	1

LEGEND

No Stitch
Placeholder—no stitch made

K
RS: Knit stitch
WS: Purl stitch

P
RS: Purl stitch
WS: Knit stitch

YO
Yarn over

Sl1, K2, PSSO
Slip 1 purl-wise, knit 2 sts, pass slip stitch over knits

BANJO
by Jenny Williams

This sweet and fun dishcloth makes the perfect gift for the music-loving person in your life! Unique cables twist and turn to create banjo shapes filled with Seed Stitch and framed by a sea of Reverse Stockinette. A Seed Stitch border surrounds and finishes the piece.

FINISHED MEASUREMENTS
9″ × 9″

YARN
Dishie™ (worsted weight, 100% Cotton; 190 yards/100g); Linen 25400, 1 skein

NEEDLES
US 5 (3.75 mm) circular or straight needles

NOTIONS
Yarn Needle

GAUGE
25 sts and 29 rows = 4″ in Banjo Chart pattern, blocked

Seed Stitch (flat over an odd number of sts)
Row 1: (K1, P1) to end.
Rep Row 1 for pattern.

DIRECTIONS
CO 58 sts.
Work Seed St for four rows.

Next Row: Work Seed St over 3 sts, work Banjo Chart sts 1–20 twice over 40 sts, work Banjo Chart sts 21–32 once, work Seed St over last 3 sts.

Cont in established pattern through Banjo Chart Row 12 five times total.

Work Seed St for four rows.
BO all sts.

Finishing
Weave in the ends. Wash and block as you like.

Banjo Chart

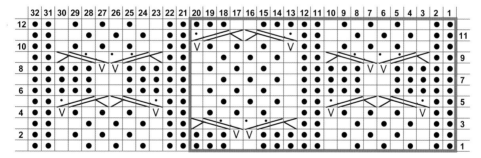

LEGEND

K
RS: Knit stitch
WS: Purl stitch

P
RS: Purl stitch
WS: Knit stitch

Sl
RS: Slip stitch purl-wise, with yarn in back
WS: Slip stitch purl-wise, with yarn in front

Pattern Repeat

Cable 1 Over 3 Right, purl back (1/3 RPC)
Sl3 to CN, hold in back; K1, P3 from CN

Cable 1 Over 3 Left, purl back (1/3 LPC)
Sl1 to CN, hold in front; P3, K1 from CN

Cable 1 Over 3 Right, rib back (1/3 RC-R)
Sl3 to CN, hold in back; K1, (P1, K1, P1) from CN

Cable 1 Over 3 Left, rib back (1/3 LC-R)
Sl1 to CN, hold in front; K1, P1, K1, K1 from CN

TWINED
by Allison Griffith

A beautiful cable winds its way up one side of this dishcloth, giving it an asymmetrical style that will look wonderful in any kitchen. This is a perfect project for a knitter wanting to practice their cable skills, as the cable repeats only every eight rows and body is simple Garter Stitch.

FINISHED MEASUREMENTS
8" square

YARN
Dishie™ (worsted weight, 100% Cotton; 190 yards/100g): Linen 25400, 1 skein

NEEDLES
US 6 (4mm) straight or circular needles

NOTIONS
Yarn Needle
Stitch Markers
Cable Needle

GAUGE
20 sts and 34 rows = 4" in Garter Stitch, lightly blocked

DIRECTIONS
CO 40 sts.
Row 1 (RS): K across.
Row 2 (WS): K10, PM, P5, PM, K to end.

Rep the following row, working Twined Cable Chart as you go. Cont until you have worked Rows 1–8 of chart eight times.
All Rows: K to marker, SM, work Twined Cable Chart, SM, K to end.

Knit one row.
BO K-wise.

Finishing
Weave in ends, wash, and block to measurements.

Twined Cable Chart

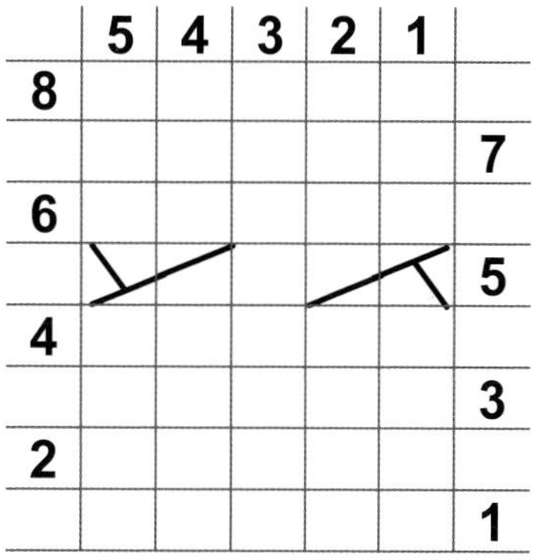

LEGEND

K
RS: Knit stitch
WS: Purl stitch

Cable 3 Over 2 Right (3/2 RC)
Sl2 to CN, hold in back; K3, K2 from CN

DAISY LACE
by Jenny Williams

While not quite as sweet as a daisy, this dishcloth is sure to make you smile. Starting with a Garter Stitch border, the daisy-inspired stitch pattern is made up of simple yarn overs and decreases, perfect for beginner knitters wanting to up their knitting game.

FINISHED MEASUREMENTS
9″ × 9.25″

YARN
Dishie™ (worsted weight, 100% Cotton; 190 yards/100g): Crème Brûlée 25404, 1 skein

NEEDLES
US 5 (3.75mm) circular or straight needles

NOTIONS
Yarn Needle

GAUGE
20 sts and 30 rows = 4″ in Daisy Lace Chart, blocked

DIRECTIONS
CO 45 sts.
Work Garter Stitch for twelve rows.

Row 1 (RS): Work Garter Stitch for 4 sts, work Daisy Lace Chart Sts 1–6 once, work Daisy Lace Chart Sts 7–18 twice, work Daisy Lace Chart Sts 19–25 once, work Garter Stitch for 4 sts.

Cont in established pattern through Daisy Lace Chart Row 24 twice.

Work Garter Stitch for twelve rows.
BO all sts.

Finishing
Weave in the ends. Block if desired.

Daisy Lace Chart

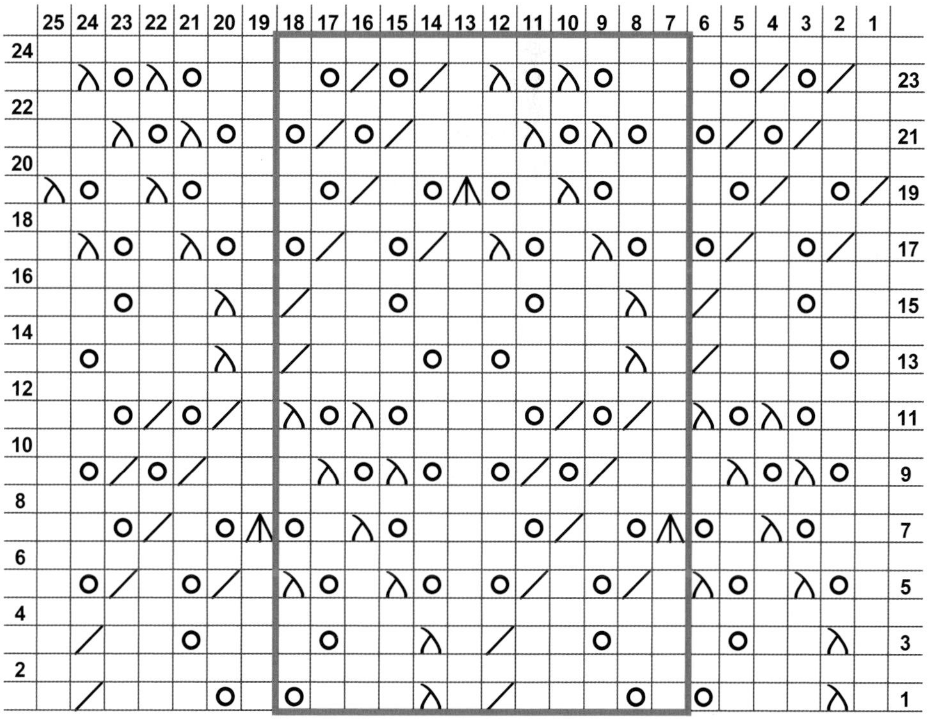

LEGEND

K
RS: Knit stitch
WS: Purl stitch

YO
Yarn over

K2tog
Knit 2 stitches together as one stitch

SKP
Slip 1 knit-wise, knit 1, pass slip stitch over knit stitch

CDD
Slip first and second stitches together as if to K2tog; knit 1 stitch; pass 2 slipped stitches over the knit stitch

Pattern Repeat

SEED STITCH CHECKS
by Knit Picks Design Team

This simple pattern works up quickly so you will have a new dishcloth in no time. The checks are made up of knits and purls, and the stitch pattern is bordered by Garter Stitch. The final project is perfect for gifts or for your own spring cleaning.

FINISHED MEASUREMENTS
8.5" square

YARN
Dishie™ (worsted weight, 100% Cotton; 190 yards/100g): Bumblebee 28096, 1 skein

NEEDLES
US 7 (4.5 mm) straight or circular needles

NOTIONS
Yarn Needle
Stitch Markers

GAUGE
18 sts and 24 rows = 4" in Seed Stitch Checks Pattern, blocked

Seed Stitch Checks (flat over a multiple of 8 sts plus 1)
Row 1 (RS): *(K1, P1) two times, K3; rep from * to last 5 sts, (K1, P1) two times, K1.
Row 2 (WS): *(K1, P1) two times, K1, P2; rep from * to last 5 sts, (K1, P1) two times, K1.
Rows 3–6: Rep Rows 1–2 two more times.
Row 7: K across.
Row 8: P across.
Rep Rows 1–8 for pattern.

DIRECTIONS
Loosely CO 41 sts.
Knit four rows.

Row 1: K4, work Row 1 of Seed Stitch Checks to last 4 sts, K4.
Row 2: K4, work Row 2 of Seed Stitch Checks to last 4 sts, K4.

Cont as established, working through Seed Stitch Checks pattern, with 4 K sts at each end.
Work until piece measures 8" from beginning, approx eight reps total, ending after a stitch pattern Row 8.

Knit four rows.
BO all sts.

Finishing
Weave in ends, wash, and block if desired.

CANDY CORN
by Stana D. Sortor

This sweet candy corn-shaped dishcloth is knit entirely in Garter Stitch. It starts at the bottom, with decrease stitches worked on the second stitch and one before the last stitch. The last stitch of every row is slipped purl-wise with yarn in front for a nice edge.

FINISHED MEASUREMENTS
8" width × 9.25" height

YARN
Dishie™ (worsted weight, 100% Cotton; 190 yards/100g): C1 Crème Brûlée 25404, C2 Clementine 25403, C3 Swan 25409, 1 skein each

NEEDLES
US 7 (4.5mm) straight or circular needles

NOTIONS
Yarn Needle
Stitch Markers

GAUGE
18 sts and 28 rows = 4" in Garter Stitch, blocked

DIRECTIONS
With C1, CO 36 sts.
Rows 1-2: K35, Sl1.
Row 3: K1, SSK, K30, K2tog, Sl1. (34 sts)
Rows 4-6: K33, Sl1.
Row 7: K1, SSK, K28, K2tog, Sl1. (32 sts)
Rows 8-10: K31, Sl1.
Row 11: K1, SSK, K26, K2tog, Sl1. (30 sts)
Rows 12-14: K29, Sl1.
Row 15: K1, SSK, K24, K2tog, Sl1. (28 sts)
Rows 16-18: K27, Sl1.
Row 19: K1, SSK, K22, K2tog, Sl1. (26 sts)
Row 20: K25, Sl1.

Break C1. Attach C2.
Rows 21-22: K25, Sl1.
Row 23 K1, SSK, K20, K2tog, Sl1. (24 sts)
Rows 24-26: K23, Sl1.
Row 27: K1, SSK, K18, K2tog, Sl1. (22 sts)
Rows 28-30: K21, Sl1.
Row 31: K1, SSK, K16, K2tog, Sl1 (20 sts)
Rows 32-34: K19, Sl1.
Row 35: K1, SSK, K14, K2tog, Sl1. (18 sts)
Rows 36-38: K17, Sl1.
Row 39: K1, SSK, K12, K2tog, Sl1. (16 sts)
Rows 40-42: K15, Sl1.
Row 43: K1, SSK, K10, K2tog, Sl1. (14 sts)
Rows 44-46: K13, Sl1.
Row 47: K1, SSK, K8, K2tog, Sl1. (12 sts)
Rows 48-50: K11, Sl1.

Break C2. Attach C3.
Row 51: K1, SSK, K6, K2tog, Sl1. (10 sts)
Rows 52-54: K9, Sl1.
Row 55: K1, SSK, K4, K2tog, Sl1. (8 sts)
Rows 56-58: K7, Sl1.
Row 59: K1, SSK, K2, K2tog, Sl1. (6 sts)
Rows 60-62: K5, Sl1.
Row 63: K1, SSK, K2tog, Sl1. (4 sts)
Row 64: K3, Sl1.
BO all sts.

Finishing
Weave in ends, wash, and block to measurements.

HONEY
by Violet LeBeaux

Honey is a simple dishcloth featuring a hexagonal shape reminiscent of honeycomb. The border is Garter Stitch and the interior is Stockinette. It includes design options for plain, striped, or embroidered versions. The design works up quickly and is lovely for spring-themed gifts.

FINISHED MEASUREMENTS
7" width at widest point × 7" height

YARN
Dishie™ (worsted weight, 100% Cotton; 190 yards/100g): MC Clementine 25403, C1 Crème Brûlée 25404, C2 Black 26669, 1 skein each

NEEDLES
US 6 (4mm) straight or circular needles

NOTIONS
Yarn Needle

GAUGE
18 sts and 24 rows = 4" in Stockinette Stitch, blocked

Color Options
Plain: Complete entire project using MC.
Striped: Begin project using MC and switch between MC and C1 every four rows. See Chart for color changes.
Embroidered: Complete project in your chosen colors, then embroider with C2 over the top. See Chart for placement.

DIRECTIONS
With MC, loosely CO 12 sts.

Row 1 (RS): K3, M1R, K to last 3 sts, M1L, K to end. 2 sts inc.
Row 2: K3, P to last 3 sts, K to end.
Rep Rows 1–2 until you have a total of 32 sts.

Row 21: K3, K2tog, K to last 5 sts, SSK, K to end. 2 sts dec.
Row 22: K3, P to last 3 sts, K to end.
Rep Rows 21–22 until a total of 12 sts remain.

BO 11 sts.

Optionally, K1 with remaining st for 2" and secure at corner to create a loop for hanging. If preferred, this can be worked as a crochet chain.

Finishing
Embroider Honey phrase referencing chart for placement. Weave in ends, wash, and block to measurements.

LEGEND

▨	Main Color (Clementine)
▢	Contrasting Color 1 (Creme Brulee)
—	Contrasting Color 2 (Black) Embroidery
■	**No Stitch** Placeholder—no stitch made
▢	**K** RS: Knit stitch WS: Purl stitch
•	**P** RS: Purl stitch WS: Knit stitch
MR	**M1R** Make 1 right-leaning stitch
ML	**M1L** Make 1 left-leaning stitch
╱	**K2tog** Knit 2 stitches together as one stitch
╲	**SSK** Slip, slip, knit slipped stitches together

Honey Chart

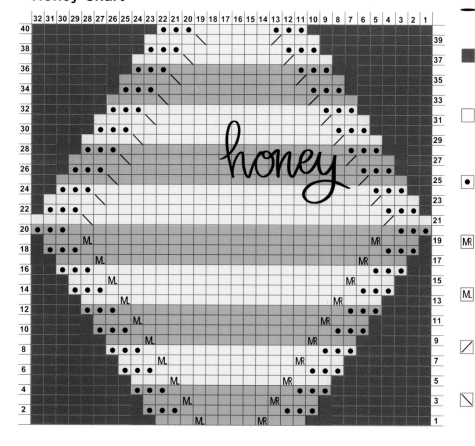

BEADED RIBS
by Faith Schmidt

The Beaded Ribs dishcloth is a quick and fun knit.
Nice and squishy, the stitch pattern is easy to memorize.
It can easily be resized to fit your needs.

FINISHED MEASUREMENTS
9" square, unblocked

YARN
Dishie™ (worsted weight, 100% Cotton;
190 yards/100g): Fox 28097, 1 skein

NEEDLES
US 5 (4.5mm) straight or circular needles

NOTIONS
Yarn Needle

GAUGE
21 sts = 4" in Beaded Ribs Stitch, unblocked and
slightly stretched

To Resize: Cast on a multiple of 8 stitches plus 1,
and knit to desired length.

Beaded Ribs Stitch (flat over a multiple of 8 sts plus 1)
Row 1 (RS): K1, (K1, P2, K1, P2, K2) to end of row.
Rows 2–4: K the knit sts and P the purl sts.
Row 5: K1, (P2, K3, P2, K1) to end of row.
Rows 6–8: K the knit sts and P the purl sts.
Rep Rows 1–8 for pattern.

DIRECTIONS
CO 49 sts, using a Long Tail Cast On.

Work Beaded Ribs Stitch pattern (Rows 1–8) seven times
total, ending the last rep on a Row 7.

BO all sts.

Finishing
Weave in ends. Block if desired.

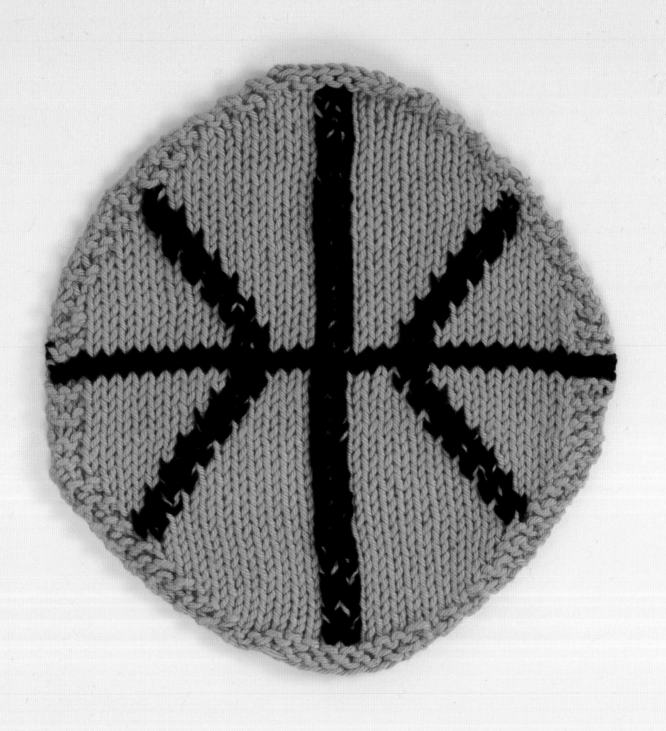

BASKETBALL
by Emily Ringelman

This washcloth is a perfect gift for that rabid NBA fan in your life!

The Basketball dishcloth is worked from the bottom up with simple shaping and has a Garter Stitch edge to prevent rolling. The central black stripe is knitted in, but the rest of the black detailing is done after the knitting is done, using duplicate stitch.

FINISHED MEASUREMENTS
7" across

YARN
Dishie™ (worsted weight, 100% Cotton; 190 yards/100g): MC Clementine 25403, CC Black 26669, 1 skein each

NEEDLES
US 7 (4.5m) straight or circular needles

NOTIONS
Yarn Needle
Stitch Markers

GAUGE
20 sts and 28 rows = 4" in Stockinette Stitch, blocked

DIRECTIONS
With MC, CO 8.
Row 1 (WS): KFB, K6, KFB. 2 sts inc.
Row 2 (RS): KFB, K8, KFB. 2 sts inc.
Row 3: KFB, K10, KFB. 2 sts inc.

Row 4: KFB, K to last 2 sts, KFB, K1. 2 sts inc.
Row 5: K1, KFB, P to last 2 sts, K1, KFB. 2 sts inc.
Rep the last two rows once more. 22 sts.

Row 8: KFB, K to last 2 sts, KFB, K1. 2 sts inc.
Row 9: K3, P to last 3 sts, K3.
Rep the last two rows six more times. 36 sts.

Row 22: K across.
Row 23: K3, P to last 3 sts, K3.
Rep the last two rows two more times.

Switch to CC, but do not break MC; carry it up side of next two rows.
Row 28: K across.
Row 29: K3, P to last 3 sts, K3.

Break CC and resume with MC.
Row 30: K across.
Row 31: K3, P to last 3 sts, K3.
Rep the last two rows two more times.

Row 36: SSK, K to last 2 sts, K2tog. 2 sts dec.
Row 37: K3, P to last 3 sts, K3.
Rep the last two rows five more times. 24 sts.

Row 48: SSK, K to last 2 sts, K2tog. 2 sts dec.
Row 49: SSK, K1, P to last 3 sts, K1, K2tog. 2 sts dec.
Rep the last two rows three more times. 8 sts.

BO K-wise.

Finishing
Weave in ends, wash, and block to a round shape.

Cut a length of CC. Following the Duplicate Stitch Chart, duplicate stitch the details onto the basketball. Weave in remaining ends and block again if desired.

Duplicate Stitch Chart

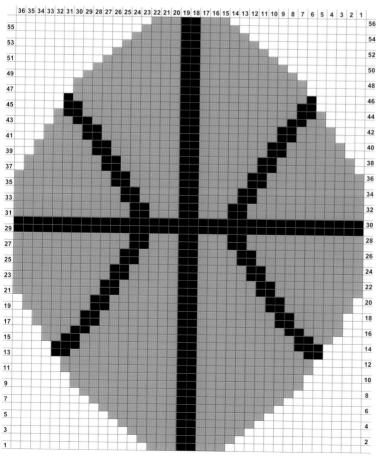

LEGEND

■ Main Color

■ Duplicate Stitch with Contrasting Color

GARTER LACE
by Knit Picks Design Team

Get a taste of lace knitting with this easy project. With a row of decreases and a row of increases separated by bands of Stockinette, this project works up quickly and is a wonderful addition to your kitchen.

FINISHED MEASUREMENTS
8.5" square

YARN
Dishie™ Twist (worsted weight, 100% Cotton; 190 yards/100g): Conch Twist 28247, 1 skein

NEEDLES
US 7 (4.5 mm) straight or circular needles

NOTIONS
Yarn Needle
Stitch Markers

GAUGE
20 sts and 28 rows = 4" in Garter Lace Pattern, blocked

Garter Lace Pattern (flat over an even number of sts)
Row 1 (RS): K across.
Row 2 (WS): (K2tog) to end.
Row 3: (KFB) to end.
Row 4: P across.
Row 5: K across.
Rows 6-7: Rep Rows 4–5.
Rows 8-9: Rep Rows 2–3.
Rows 10: P across.
Rep Rows 1–10 for pattern.

DIRECTIONS
Loosely CO 44 sts.
Knit four rows.

Row 1: K4, work Row 1 of Garter Lace Pattern to last 4 sts, K4.
Row 2: K4, work Row 2 of Garter Lace Pattern to last 4 sts, K4.

Cont as established, working through Garter Lace Pattern rows, with 4 knit sts at each end of each row.
Work until piece measures 8" from CO edge, ending after a stitch pattern Row 10.

Knit four rows.
BO all sts.

Finishing
Weave in ends, wash, and block if desired.

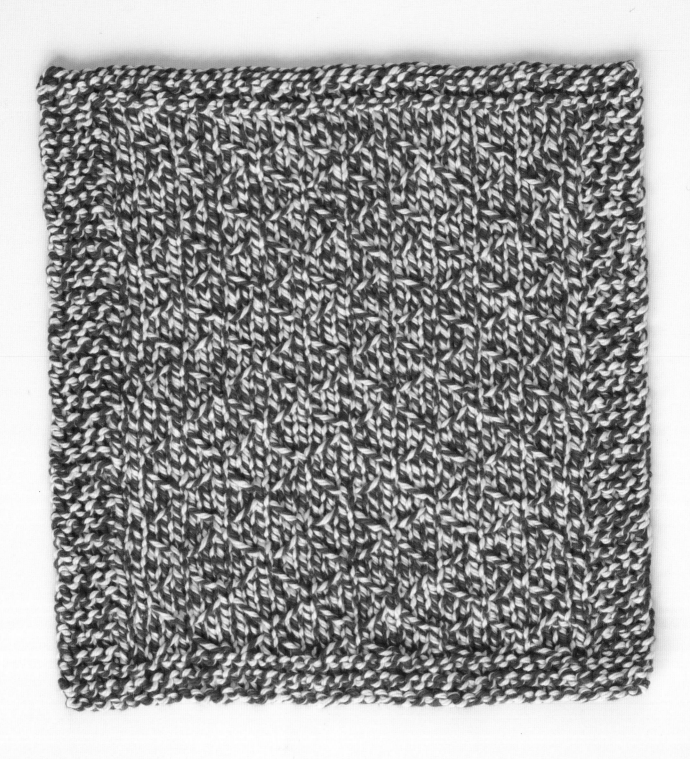

LINKS
by Knit Picks Design Team

This pretty pattern resembles a chain link fence when complete! Use a solid color to see the pattern more clearly, or a marled or multi-colored yarn to get a fun texture on your dishcloth.

This stitch pattern is made by bringing the working yarn in front of the slipped stitches, then back to the back, creating a float. On the next right side, the float is lifted up and brought behind the next stitch.

FINISHED MEASUREMENTS
8.5" square

YARN
Dishie™ Twist (worsted weight, 100% Cotton; 190 yards/100g): Fiesta Red Twist 28248, 1 skein

NEEDLES
US 7 (4.5 mm) straight or circular needles

NOTIONS
Yarn Needle
Stitch Markers

GAUGE
19 sts and 32 rows = 4" in Chain Link Pattern, blocked

KU (knit under strand)
Insert RH needle under float from previous row, knit next st, bring RH needle back under float.

Chain Link Pattern (flat over a multiple of 6 sts plus 3)
Row 1 (RS): K2, (WYIF Sl5 P-wise, K1) to last st, K1.
Row 2 and all WS rows: P across.
Row 3: K4, (KU, K5) to end (ending K4).
Row 5: K1, WYIF Sl3 P-wise, (K1, WYIF Sl5 P-wise) to last 5 sts, K1, WYIF Sl3 P-wise, K1.
Row 7: K1, (KU, K5) to last 2 sts, KU, K1.
Row 8: P across.
Rep Rows 1–8 for pattern.

DIRECTIONS
Loosely CO 41 sts.
Knit four rows.
Purl one row

Row 1 (RS): K4, work Row 1 of Chain Link Pattern to last 4 sts, K4.
Row 2 (WS): K4, work Row 2 of Chain Link Pattern to last 4 sts, K4.

Cont as established, working through Chain Link Pattern rows, with 4 knit sts at each end.
Work until piece measures 8" from CO edge, ending after a stitch pattern Row 8.

Knit four rows.
BO all sts.

Finishing
Weave in ends, wash, and block if desired.

PEPPERMINT CANDY
by Knit Picks Design Team

The holidays just aren't complete without peppermint candy! This dishcloth uses matching red and white colors to create a subtle design evoking the classic hard candy. Using mosaic knitting technique, only one color is used per row for the main stitch pattern, with slip stitches creating the fun shapes. A Garter Stitch border completes this festive project, perfect for getting into the holiday spirit.

All stitches are slipped purl-wise, with yarn in back on the right side and yarn in front on the wrong side. Before beginning, wind a second ball of the main color yarn—this is used to create a seamless border. Do not break the unused color when switching to a new color in the stitch pattern; instead, carry it up the wrong side so there will not be as many ends to weave in.

FINISHED MEASUREMENTS
8.5″ square

YARN
Dishie™ (worsted weight, 100% Cotton; 190 yards/100g): MC Fiesta Red 25786, CC Fiesta Red Twist 28248, 1 skein each

NEEDLES
US 7 (4.5 mm) straight or circular needles

NOTIONS
Yarn Needle
Stitch Markers

GAUGE
20 sts and 24 rows = 4″ in Mosaic Pattern, blocked

Mosaic Pattern (flat over 4 sts plus 3)
Row 1 (RS): With CC, K1, (Sl1 WYIB, K3) to last 2 sts, Sl1 WYIB, K1.
Row 2 (WS): With CC, K1, (Sl1 WYIF, K3) to last 2 sts, Sl1 WYIF, K1.
Rows 3–4: Rep Rows 1–2 in CC.
Row 5: With MC, K3, (Sl1 WYIB, K3) to end.
Row 6: With MC, K3, (Sl1 WYIF, K3) to end.
Rows 7–8: Rep Rows 5–6 in MC.
Rep Rows 1–8 for pattern.

DIRECTIONS
With MC, loosely CO 43 sts.
Knit four rows.

Row 1 (RS): K4 with MC, work Row 1 of Mosaic Pattern to last 4 sts, attach second ball of MC and K4.
Row 2 (WS): K4 with MC, work Row 2 of Mosaic Pattern to last 4 sts, K4 with MC.

Cont as established, working through Mosaic Pattern, with 4 MC knit sts at each end. Work until piece measures 8″ from CO edge, ending after a Row 4.

Knit four rows.
BO all sts.

Finishing
Weave in ends, wash, and block if desired.

APPLE
by Stana D. Sortor

An apple-shaped dishcloth with stem and a small leaf is a perfect gift for teachers, or anyone on your gift list.

This dishcloth is knit in seed stitch, starting at the bottom with one half, then stitches are held until the second half is worked, and finally both are joined. The first stitch of every row is knit while the last stitch at every row is slipped for a nice edge. The top is worked the same as the bottom. The stem and the leaf are knit separately and sewn onto the dishcloth.

FINISHED MEASUREMENTS
8.5″ width × 8″ length

YARN
Dishie™ (worsted weight, 100% Cotton; 190 yards/100g): MC Fiesta Red 25786, C1 Coffee 25399, C2 Jalapeño 25785, 1 skein each

NEEDLES
US 7 (4.5mm) straight or circular needles and DPNs

NOTIONS
Yarn Needle
Stitch Markers

GAUGE
17 sts and 28 rows = 4″ in Seed Stitch, blocked

I-Cord
With DPN, CO 3 sts. *Without turning work, slide the sts to other end of the needle, pull yarn snugly across the back of work, K3; rep from * until cord reaches desired length.

Sl1 for both RS and WS: Slip stitch P-wise, with yarn in front.

DIRECTIONS

Apple

Part 1
With MC, CO 8 sts.
Row 1: (K1, P1) three times, Sl1.
Row 2: K1 (K1, P1) three times, Sl1.
Row 3: K1, KFB, (K1, P1) two times, KFB, Sl1. 10 sts.
Row 4: K1, (P1, K1) four times, Sl1.
Break yarn and place all sts onto scrap yarn or st holder.

Part 2
With MC, CO 8 sts.
Row 1: (K1, P1) three times, Sl1.
Row 2: K1 (K1, P1) three times, Sl1.
Row 3: K1, KFB, (K1, P1) two times, KFB, Sl1. 10 sts.
Row 4: K1, (P1, K1) four times, Sl1.

Increase Section
On the next row, work Part 2 sts, then carefully transfer Part 1 sts onto LH needle, and cont across the two pieces, joining them tog.

Row 5: K1, KFB, (P1, K1) eight times, KFB, Sl1. 22 sts.
Row 6: K1, KFB, (P1, K1) nine times, KFB, Sl1. 24 sts.
Row 7: K1, KFB, (P1, K1) ten times, KFB, Sl1. 26 sts.
Row 8: K1, (K1, P1) twelve times, Sl1.
Row 9: K1, KFB, (K1, P1) eleven times, KFB, Sl1. 28 sts.
Row 10: (K1, P1) 13 times, K1, Sl1.
Row 11: K1 (K1, P1) 13 times, Sl1.
Row 12: Rep Row 10.
Row 13: K1, KFB, (P1, K1) twelve times, KFB, Sl1. 30 sts.
Row 14: K1 (K1, P1) 14 times, Sl1.
Row 15: (K1, P1) 14 times, K1, Sl1.
Rows 16-17: Rep Rows 14-15.
Row 18: Rep Row 14.
Row 19: K1, KFB, (K1, P1) 13 times, KFB, Sl1. 32 sts.
Row 20: (K1, P1) 15 times, K1, Sl1.
Row 21: K1 (K1, P1) 15 times, Sl1.
Row 22: Rep Row 20.
Row 23: K1, KFB, (K1, P1) 14 times, KFB, Sl1. 34 sts.
Row 24: K1 (K1, P1) 16 times, Sl1.
Row 25: (K1, P1) 16 times, K1, Sl1.
Row 26-27: Rep Rows 24-25.
Row 28: K1 (K1, P1) 14 times, Sl1.
Row 29: K1, KFB, (K1, P1) 15 times, KFB, Sl1. 36 sts.
Row 30: (K1, P1) 17 times, K1, Sl1.
Row 31: K1 (K1, P1) 17 times, Sl1.
Row 32-33: Rep Rows 30-31.
Row 34: Rep Row 30.

Decrease Section
Row 35: K1, SSK, (K1, P1) 15 times, K2tog, Sl1. 34 sts.
Row 36: K1 (K1, P1) 16 times, Sl1.
Row 37: (K1, P1) 16 times, K1, Sl1.
Row 38: Rep Row 36.

Row 39: K1, SSK, (P1, K1) 14 times, K2tog, Sl1. 32 sts.
Row 40: (K1, P1) 15 times, K1, Sl1.
Row 41: K1 (K1, P1) 15 times, Sl1.
Row 42: Rep Row 40.
Row 43: K1, SSK, (P1, K1) 13 times, K2tog, Sl1. 30 sts.
Row 44: K1 (K1, P1) 14 times, Sl1.
Row 45: (K1, P1) 14 times, K1, Sl1.
Row 46: Rep Row 44.
Row 47: K1, SSK, (P1, K1) twelve times, K2tog, Sl1. 28 sts.
Row 48: (K1, P1) 13 times, K1, Sl1.
Row 49: K1 (K1, P1) 13 times, Sl1.
Row 50: Rep Row 48.
Row 51: K1, SSK, (K1, P1) five times, BO 2 sts, P1, (K1, P1) four times, K2tog, Sl1. 24 sts total.

Left Side

Cont with second half of Apple. Leave first half to work later.
Row 52: K1 (K1, P1) five times, Sl1. 12 sts.
Row 53: (K1, P1) five times, K1, Sl1.
Row 54: K1, (P1, K1) five times, Sl1.
Row 55: K1, SSK, (P1, K1) three times, K2tog, Sl1. 10 sts.
Row 56: (K1, P1) four times, K1, Sl1.
BO in (K1, P1) pattern.

Right Side

Attach MC to middle of top of Apple. Cont with first half of Apple.
Row 52: K1 (K1, P1) five times, Sl1. 12 sts.
Row 53: (K1, P1) five times, K1, Sl1.

Row 54: K1, (P1, K1) five times, Sl1.
Row 55: K1, SSK, (P1, K1) three times, K2tog, Sl1. 10 sts.
Row 56: (K1, P1) four times, K1, Sl1.
BO in (K1, P1) pattern.

Stem

With C1, CO 3 sts. Work I-cord for ten rows.
Break yarn, leaving long tail, and thread tail onto a yarn needle. Pull end through remaining st on needles to close hole and stitch to secure.

Leaf

With C2, CO 3 sts.
Rows 1–2: K2, Sl1.
Row 3: (KFB) two times, Sl1. 5 sts.
Row 4: K4, Sl1.
Row 5: (K1, KFB) two times, Sl1. 7 sts.
Row 6: K6, Sl1.
Row 7: K1, SSK, K1, K2tog, Sl1. 5 sts.
Row 8: K4, Sl1.
Row 9: SSK, K1, K2tog, Sl1. 3 sts.
Row 10: K2, Sl1.
Row 11: K3tog. 1 st.
Break yarn, leaving long tail. Thread tail onto yarn needle, then pull through remaining st, pulling tightly to close hole.

Finishing

Sew leaf to stem, then attach stem to center of top of apple. Weave in ends, wash, and block to measurements.

LACE HEART
by Jenny Williams

A project to make for someone you love, or just add some love to your own kitchen! Garter Stitch and Stockinette Stitch are used to frame the lace heart, which is made up of yarn overs and decreases.

FINISHED MEASUREMENTS
9.25" square

YARN
Dishie™ (worsted weight, 100% Cotton; 190 yards/100g); Begonia 25790, 1 skein

NEEDLES
US 5 (3.75mm) circular or straight needles

NOTIONS
Yarn Needle

GAUGE
19 sts and 30 rows = 4" in Lace Heart Chart, blocked

DIRECTIONS
CO 47 sts.

Row 1 (RS): Work Lace Heart Chart (next page) Row 1. Cont in established pattern through Lace Heart Chart Row 74.

BO all sts.

Finishing
Weave in the ends and wash.

Lace Heart Chart

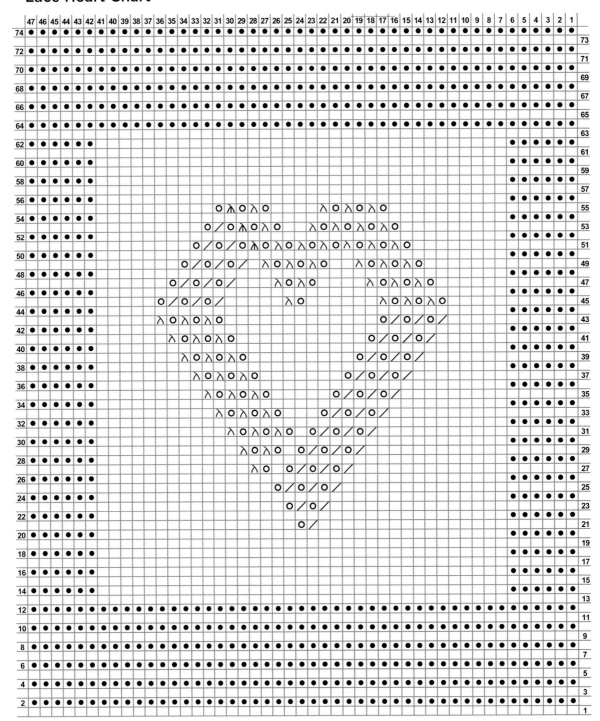

LEGEND

K
RS: Knit stitch
WS: Purl stitch

P
RS: Purl stitch
WS: Knit stitch

YO
Yarn over

K2tog
Knit 2 stitches together as one stitch

SKP
Slip 1 knit-wise, knit 1, pass slip stitch over knit stitch

SK2P
Slip 1 knit-wise, K2tog, pass slip stitch over K2tog

STRAWBERRY TWIST
by Stana D. Sortor

Harken back to summers gone by with this sweet dishcloth. Inspired by a favorite childhood treat, this project features cables twisting their way through the dishcloth. Easy and fun, you'll want to relive the magic again and again.

This simple, square dishcloth starts with a ribbed pattern, with three large cables across the body. The last stitch of each row is slipped, creating a tidy edge.

FINISHED MEASUREMENTS
8" square

YARN
Shine™ (sport weight, 60% Pima Cotton, 40% Modal; 110 yards/50g): Blush 23614, 1 skein

NEEDLES
US 5 (3.75mm) straight or circular needles

NOTIONS
Yarn Needle
Stitch Markers
Cable Needle

GAUGE
28 sts and 32 rows = 4" in Stockinette Stitch, blocked

5/5 RC (cable 5 over 5 right)
Sl5 sts to CN, hold in back, K5; K5 from CN.

5/5 LC (cable 5 over 5 left)
Sl5 sts to CN, hold in front, K5; K5 from CN.

4/4 RC (cable 4 over 4 right)
Sl4 sts to CN, hold in back, K4; K4 from CN.

4/4 LC (cable 4 over 4 left)
Sl4 sts to CN, hold in front, K4; K4 from CN.

DIRECTIONS

CO 58 sts.
Work from Strawberry Twist Chart (next page) or follow the written directions here.

Row 1: (K2, P2) 14 times, K1, Sl1 WYIF.
Row 2: (P2, K2) 14 times, P1, Sl1 WYIF.
Rows 3-6: Rep Rows 1-2.
Row 7: (K2, P2) two times, K10, P3, K16, P3, K10, P2, K2, P2, K1, Sl1 WYIF.
Row 8: (P2, K2) two times, P10, K3, P16, K3, P10, K2, P2, K2, P1, Sl1 WYIF.
Row 9: (K2, P2) two times, K10, P3, K16, P3, K10, P2, K2, P2, K1, Sl1 WYIF.
Row 10: Rep Row 8.
Row 11: (K2, P2) two times, RC 5/5, P3, RC 4/4, LC 4/4, P3, LC 5/5, P2, K2, P2, K1, Sl1 WYIF.
Rows 12-18: Rep Rows 8-9.
Row 19: (K2, P2) two times, K10, P3, RC 4/4, LC 4/4, P3, K10, P2, K2, P2, K1, Sl1 WYIF.
Row 20: Rep Row 8.
Row 21: (K2, P2) two times, RC 5/5, P3, K16, P3, LC5/5, P2, K2, P2, K1, Sl1 WYIF.
Rows 22-26: Rep Rows 8-9.
Row 27: Rep Row 19.
Rows 28-30: Rep Rows 8-9.
Row 31: Rep Row 21.
Rows 32-34: Rep Rows 8-9.
Row 35: Rep Row 19.
Rows 36-40: Rep Rows 8-9.
Row 41: Rep Row 21.
Row 42: Rep Row 8.
Row 43: Rep Row 19.
Rows 44-50: Rep Rows 8-9.
Row 51: Rep Row 11.
Rows 52-56: Rep Rows 8-9.
Rows 57-62: Rep Rows 1-2.

BO in 2x2 Rib.

Finishing
Weave in ends, wash, and block to measurements.

Strawberry Twist Chart

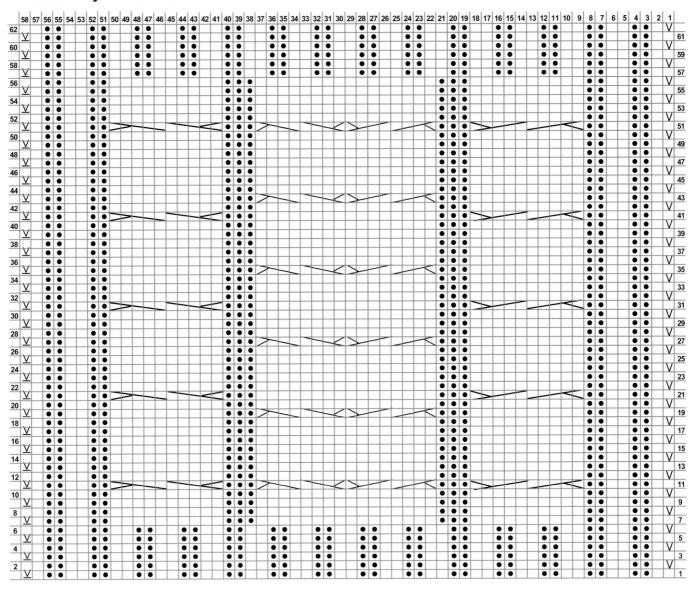

LEGEND

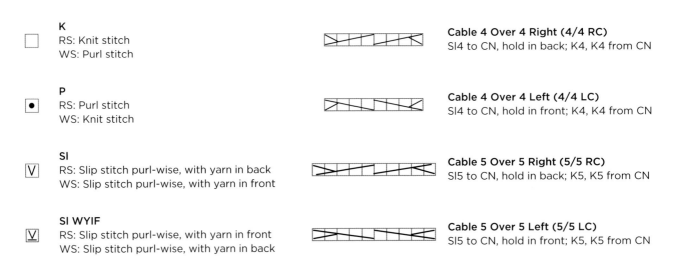

K
RS: Knit stitch
WS: Purl stitch

P
RS: Purl stitch
WS: Knit stitch

Sl
RS: Slip stitch purl-wise, with yarn in back
WS: Slip stitch purl-wise, with yarn in front

Sl WYIF
RS: Slip stitch purl-wise, with yarn in front
WS: Slip stitch purl-wise, with yarn in back

Cable 4 Over 4 Right (4/4 RC)
Sl4 to CN, hold in back; K4, K4 from CN

Cable 4 Over 4 Left (4/4 LC)
Sl4 to CN, hold in front; K4, K4 from CN

Cable 5 Over 5 Right (5/5 RC)
Sl5 to CN, hold in back; K5, K5 from CN

Cable 5 Over 5 Left (5/5 LC)
Sl5 to CN, hold in front; K5, K5 from CN

VERTICAL WRAPPED STITCH
by Jenny Williams

If you are looking for a dishcloth with heavy scrubbing power, you can't go wrong with this project. The Vertical Wrapped Stitch dishcloth features an easy to memorize stitch pattern that creates a dense fabric that is completely reversible. You'll want one in every color!

FINISHED MEASUREMENTS

9" square

YARN

Dishie™ (worsted weight, 100% Cotton; 190 yards/100g); Blush 26668, 1 skein

NEEDLES

US 5 (3.75mm) circular or straight needles

NOTIONS

Yarn Needle

GAUGE

20 sts and 30 rows = 4" in stitch pattern, blocked

Always slip stitches purl-wise.

K2tog TBL decreases are always worked with the slipped stitch and the yarn over loop knit together.

DIRECTIONS

CO 47 sts.

Row 1 (WS): K1, (YO, Sl1 WYIB, K1) to end.
Row 2 (RS): K1, (K2tog TBL, K1) to end.
Rep Rows 1–2 for 9".

BO all sts.

Finishing

Weave in the ends and wash.

ARROW
by Violet LeBeaux

Arrow is a cabled dishcloth featuring an arrow design made with easy mini-cables. It's perfect paired with a heart on Valentine's Day or in a neutral color alone. The dishcloth has a garter stitch border and reverse stockinette around the cabled arrow.

FINISHED MEASUREMENTS
7.25″ width × 7.5″ height

YARN
Dishie™ (worsted weight, 100% Cotton; 190 yards/100g): Blush 26668, 1 skein

NEEDLES
US 6 (4mm) straight or circular needles

NOTIONS
Yarn Needle
2 Cable Needles

GAUGE
18 sts and 24 rows = 4″ in Reverse Stockinette Stitch, blocked
18 sts and 40 rows = 4″ in Garter Stitch, blocked

LTP (left twist, purl back)
RS: Sl next st onto CN, hold in front, P next st from LH needle, K st from CN.
WS: Sl next st onto CN, hold in back, K next st from LH needle, P st from CN.

RTP (right twist, purl back)
RS: Sl next st onto CN, hold in back, K next st from LH needle, P st from CN.
WS: Sl next st onto CN, hold in front, P next st from LH needle, K st from CN.

PT (point twist)
RS: Sl next st onto CN, hold in back, Sl next st onto CN, hold in front, P next st from LH needle, K st from front CN, P st from back CN.
WS: Sl next st onto CN, hold in front, Sl next st onto CN, hold in back, K next st from LH needle, P st from back CN, K st from front CN.

Arrow Stitch Pattern (flat over 13 sts)
(chart on next page)
Row 1 (RS): LTP, P9, RTP.
Row 2 (WS): K1, RTP, K7, LTP, K1.
Row 3: P2, LTP, P5, RTP, P2.
Row 4: RTP, K1, RTP, K3, LTP, K1, LTP.
Row 5: P1, LTP, p1, LTP, P1, RTP, P1, RTP, P1.
Row 6: K2, RTP, K1, PT, K1, LTP, K2.
Row 7: LTP, P1, LTP, P1, K1, P1, RTP, P1, RTP.
Row 8: K1, RTP, K1, RTP, P1, LTP, K1, LTP, K1.
Row 9: P2, LTP, P1, PT, P1, RTP, P2.
Row 10: K3, RTP, K1, P1, K1, LTP, K3.
Row 11: P4, LTP, K1, RTP, P4.
Row 12: K5, PT, K5.
Row 13: P6, K1, P6.
Row 14: K6, P1, K6.
Rep Rows 13–14 three more times.
Row 21: LTP, K9, RTP.
Row 22: K1, RTP, P7, LTP, K1.
Row 23: P2, LTP, K5, RTP, P2.
Row 24: K3, RTP, P3, LTP, K3.
Row 25: P4, LTP, K1, RTP, P4.
Row 26: K5, PT, K5.

DIRECTIONS
Loosely CO 33 sts.
Rows 1–6: K across.

Row 7 (RS): K4, P to last 4 sts, K4.
Row 8: K3, P1, K to last 4 sts, P1, K3.
Rep Rows 7–8 two more times.

Row 13: K4, P6, work Arrow Pattern starting from Row 1, P to last 4 sts, K4.
Row 14: K3, P1, K6, work Arrow Pattern, K to last 4 sts, P1, K3.
Rep Rows 13–14 twelve more times or until you have worked through the Arrow Pattern once.

Rep Rows 7–8 three times.
Next 6 Rows: K across.
BO all sts.

Finishing
Weave in ends, wash, and block to measurements.

Arrow Stitch Pattern

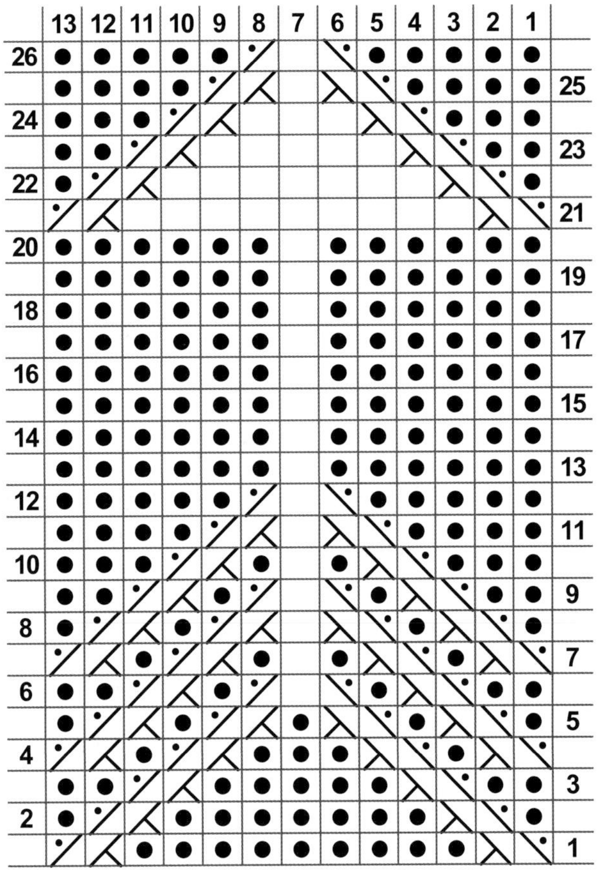

LEGEND

K
RS: Knit stitch
WS: Purl stitch

P
RS: Purl stitch
WS: Knit stitch

Right Twist, Purl back (RPT)
RS: Sl1 to CN, hold in back; K1, P1 from CN
WS: Sl1 to CN, hold in front; P1, K1 from CN

Left Twist, Purl back (LPT)
RS: Sl1 to CN, hold in front; P1, K1 from CN
WS: Sl1 to CN, hold in back; K1, P1 from CN

Point twist purl (PT)
RS: Sl1 to CN, hold in back, Sl1 to CN, hold in front; P1, K1 from front CN, P1 from back CN
WS: Sl1 to CN, hold in front, Sl1 to CN, hold in back; K1, P1 from back CN, K1 from front CN

UNSPOOLED
by Allison Griffith

Calling all sewists! Celebrate your craft with this adorable dishcloth, featuring a fun spool design. Knit up several in different colors to give as gifts!

This dishcloth is worked flat, from the bottom up. The spool is worked in Seed Stitch and the thread is worked in Garter Stitch.

FINISHED MEASUREMENTS
8″ height × 7″ width

YARN
Dishie™ (worsted weight, 100% Cotton; 190 yards/100g): MC Blush 26668, CC Coffee 25399, 1 skein each

NEEDLES
US 6 (4mm) straight or circular needles

NOTIONS
Yarn Needle

GAUGE
20 sts and 34 rows = 4″ in Garter Stitch, lightly blocked

Seed Stitch (flat over an even number of stitches)
Row 1: (K1, P1) to end.
Row 2: (P1, K1) to end.

DIRECTIONS

Spool Bottom
With CC, CO 34 sts and work flat.
Rows 1–4: Work Seed Stitch.
Rows 5–6: SSK, work Seed Stitch to end.
Rows 7–8: BO 2 sts, work Seed Stitch to end.
Break CC. 28 sts remain.

Thread
Join MC. Work Garter Stitch for 52 rows, ending with a WS row.
Break MC.

Spool Top
Join CC.
Row 1: K to end, CO 2 sts using Backward Loop Cast On.
Row 2: Work Seed Stitch to end, CO 2 sts using Backward Loop Cast On.
Rows 3–4: Work Seed Stitch to last st, KFB.
Rows 5–8: Work Seed Stitch.

BO all sts in pattern.

Finishing
Weave in ends, wash, and block to measurements.

EUHEDRAL
by Joyce Fassbender

Named for euhedral crystals, this dishcloth features a striking design of lace and texture with a Garter Stitch border. It's is an excellent project for beginners looking to level up their knitting.

FINISHED MEASUREMENTS
8.5″ width × 8″ height

YARN
Dishie™ (worsted weight, 100% Cotton; 190 yards/100g): Lilac Mist 27038, 1 skein

NEEDLES
US 7 (4.5mm) straight or circular needles

NOTIONS
Yarn Needle

GAUGE
18 sts and 24 rows = 4″ in Stockinette Stitch

DIRECTIONS

CO 39 sts using a Long Tail Cast On.

Setup Rows 1–5: K across.
Setup Row 6: K5, (YO, SSK, K5, K2tog, YO, K1) three times, K4.
Setup Row 7: K3, P1, (P5, K1, P4) three times, P2, K3.

Work Rows 1–16 of Euhedral Chart two times. Work boxed rep pattern three times per row.

Work Rows 1–15 of chart one time.
Knit across for five rows.
BO all sts.

Finishing
Weave in ends, wash, and block.

LEGEND

☐ **K**
RS: Knit stitch
WS: Purl stitch

⊡ **P**
RS: Purl stitch
WS: Knit stitch

☉ **YO**
Yarn over

◪ **K2tog**
Knit 2 stitches together as one stitch

◩ **SSK**
Slip, slip, knit slipped stitches together

☐ **Pattern Repeat**

Euhedral Chart

	19	18	17	16	15	14	13	12	11	10	9	8	7	6	5	4	3	2	1	
16	●	●	●							●							●	●	●	
					O	/				●			\	O			●	●	●	15
14	●	●	●							●							●	●	●	
					O	/		O	/		\	O			O	/	●	●	●	13
12	●	●	●						●	●	●			●			●	●	●	
							O	/				\	O				●	●	●	11
10	●	●	●					●	●	●	●	●					●	●	●	
							O	/				\	O				●	●	●	9
8	●	●	●				●	●	●	●	●	●	●				●	●	●	
																				7
6	●	●	●					●	●	●	●	●	●	●			●	●	●	
						\	O					O	/				●	●	●	5
4	●	●	●				●	●	●	●	●						●	●	●	
						\	O				O	/					●	●	●	3
2	●	●	●						●	●	●						●	●	●	
					O	/	\	O				O	/		O	/	●	●	●	1

LACE BUTTERFLY
by Jenny Williams

Decorate a simple dishcloth with a pretty butterfly made of lace! Garter Stitch and Stockinette Stitch are used to frame the lace butterfly, which is made up of yarn overs, decreases, wrapped stitches, and a bobble.

FINISHED MEASUREMENTS
9.25" square

YARN
Dishie™ (worsted weight, 100% Cotton; 190 yards/100g): Lilac Mist 27038, 1 skein

NEEDLES
US 5 (3.75mm) circular or straight needles

NOTIONS
Yarn Needle

GAUGE
19 sts and 30 rows = 4" in Lace Butterfly Chart pattern, blocked

DIRECTIONS
CO 47 sts.

Row 1 (RS): Work Lace Butterfly Chart (next page) Row 1. Cont in established pattern through Lace Butterfly Chart Row 74.

BO all sts.

Finishing
Weave in ends, wash, and block as you like.

Lace Butterfly Chart

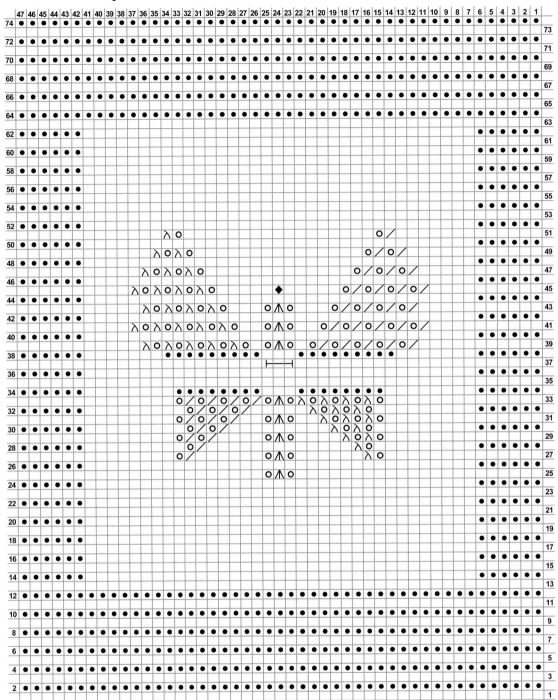

LEGEND

K
RS: Knit stitch
WS: Purl stitch

P
RS: Purl stitch
WS: Knit stitch

YO
Yarn over

K2tog
Knit 2 stitches together as one stitch

SKP
Slip 1 knit-wise, knit 1, pass slip stitch over knit stitch

CDD
Slip first and second stitches together as if to K2tog; knit 1 stitch; pass 2 slipped stitches over the knit stitch

3-Stitch Wrap
Sl3 to CN, wrap yarn around the 3 stitches counterclockwise five times, Sl stitches back to right-hand needle

Bobble
(K1, P1, K1, P1, K1) into one stitch, turn, P5, turn, Sl 2nd, 3rd, 4th & 5th stitches over 1st stitch, knit through back loop

LACY WAVES
by Faith Schmidt

The Lacy Waves dishcloth is a fun and quick knit and would make a lovely gift. The lace pattern is easy to knit and highlights the Dishie Multi. It can easily be resized to fit your needs.

FINISHED MEASUREMENTS
7.5" × 8"

YARN
Dishie™ Multi (worsted weight, 100% Cotton; 190 yards/100g): Grape Purple 27337, 1 skein

NEEDLES
US 7 (4.5 mm) straight or circular needles

NOTIONS
Yarn Needle

GAUGE
21 sts and 23 rows = 4" in Lacy Waves Pattern, unblocked

To Resize: Cast on a multiple of 18 stitches plus 4, and work to desired length.

Lacy Waves Pattern (flat over a multiple of 18 sts plus 4)
Row 1 (RS): K2, *(K2tog) three times, (K1, YO) six times, (K2tog) three times; rep from * to last 2 sts, K2.
Row 2 (WS): K2, P to last 2 sts, K2.
Row 3: K2, *(K2tog) three times, (K1, YO) six times, (K2tog) three times; rep from * to last 2 sts, K2.
Row 4: K2, P to last 2 sts, K2.
Row 5: K across.
Row 6: K across.
Row 7: K2, P to last 2 sts, K2.
Row 8: K across.
Rep Rows 1–8 for pattern.

DIRECTIONS
CO 40 sts, using a Long Tail Cast On.
Knit three rows.

Work Lacy Waves Pattern (Rows 1–8) five times.

Rep Rows 1–6 once more.
BO all sts.

Finishing
Weave in ends. Block, if desired.

NETWORK
by Violet LeBeaux

Network is a simple mesh lace dishcloth featuring a beginner-friendly stitch repeat. It has a garter stitch border and looks great in multi-colored and variegated yarns. The lace makes it a great kitchen scrubbing cloth.

FINISHED MEASUREMENTS
7.25″ square

YARN
Dishie™ Multi (worsted weight, 100% Cotton; 190 yards/100g): Grape Purple 27337, 1 skein

NEEDLES
US 6 (4mm) straight or circular needles

NOTIONS
Yarn Needle

GAUGE
18 sts and 24 rows = 4″ in Network Lace Pattern, blocked (gauge is approximate as the lace has a lot of stretch)
18 sts and 40 rows = 4″ in Garter Stitch, blocked

Network Lace Pattern (flat over a multiple of 2 sts)
Row 1 (RS): (K2tog, YO) to end.
Row 2 (WS): P across.
Row 3: (YO, SSK) to end.
Row 4: P across.

DIRECTIONS
Loosely CO 32 sts.
Rows 1–6: K across.

Row 7: K3, (work Network Lace Pattern starting from Row 1) to last 3 sts, K3.
Rep Row 7 35 more times or until desired length is reached.

Next 6 Rows: K across.
BO all sts.

Finishing
Weave in ends, wash, and block to measurements.

Network Lace Pattern

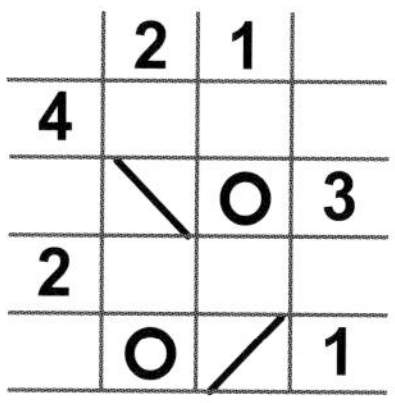

LEGEND

K
RS: Knit stitch
WS: Purl stitch

YO
Yarn over

K2tog
Knit 2 stitches together as one stitch

SSK
Slip, slip, knit slipped stitches together

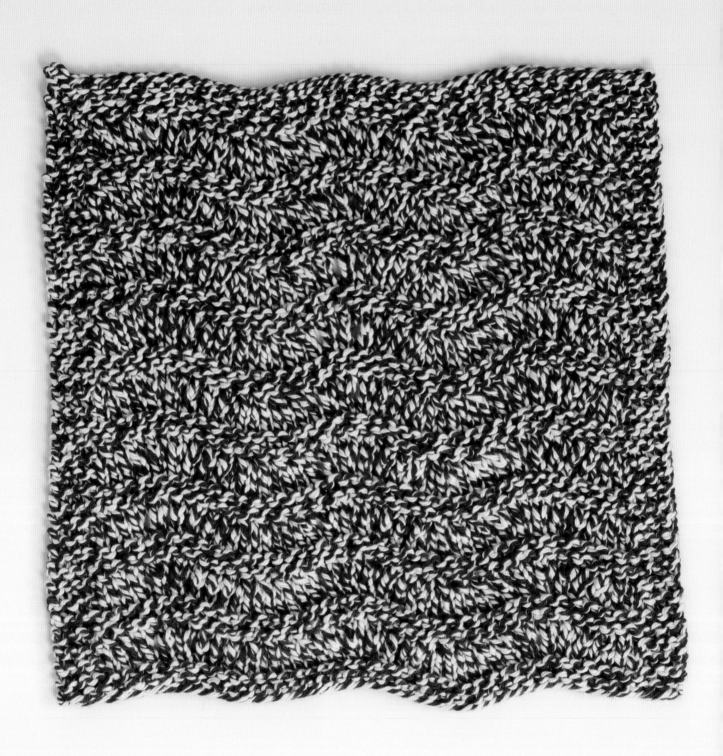

RIPPLES & RIDGES
by Knit Picks Design Team

This fast and fun dishcloth features a simple stitch pattern of Stockinette, increases, and decreases, creating a sea of ripples and ridges across the surface. With a Garter Stitch border on all sides, it's the perfect project to take a beginner to the next level of knitting skills.

FINISHED MEASUREMENTS
10.5" square

YARN
Dishie™ Twist (worsted weight, 100% Cotton; 190 yards/100g): Mulberry Twist 28251, 1 skein

NEEDLES
US 7 (4.5 mm) straight or circular needles

NOTIONS
Yarn Needle
Stitch Markers

GAUGE
18 sts and 28 rows = 4" in Ripples & Ridges Pattern, blocked

Ripples & Ridges Pattern (flat over a multiple of 13 sts)
Row 1 (RS): K across.
Rows 2–3: Rep Row 1.
Row 4: P across.
Row 5: *K4, (YO, K1) five times, YO, K4; rep from * to end.
Row 6: P across.
Row 7: *(K2tog) three times, K7, (SSK) three times; rep from * to end.
Row 8: K across.
Rep Rows 1–8 for pattern.

DIRECTIONS
Loosely CO 47 sts.
Knit one row.

Row 1 (RS): K4, work Row 1 of Ripples & Ridges Pattern to last 4 sts, K4.
Row 2 (WS): K4, work Row 2 of Ripples & Ridges Pattern to last 4 sts, K4.

Cont as established, working through Ripples & Ridges Pattern rows, with 4 knit sts at each end.
Work until piece measures 10.5" from CO edge; end after a Row 3.

BO all sts.

Finishing
Weave in ends, wash, and block if desired.

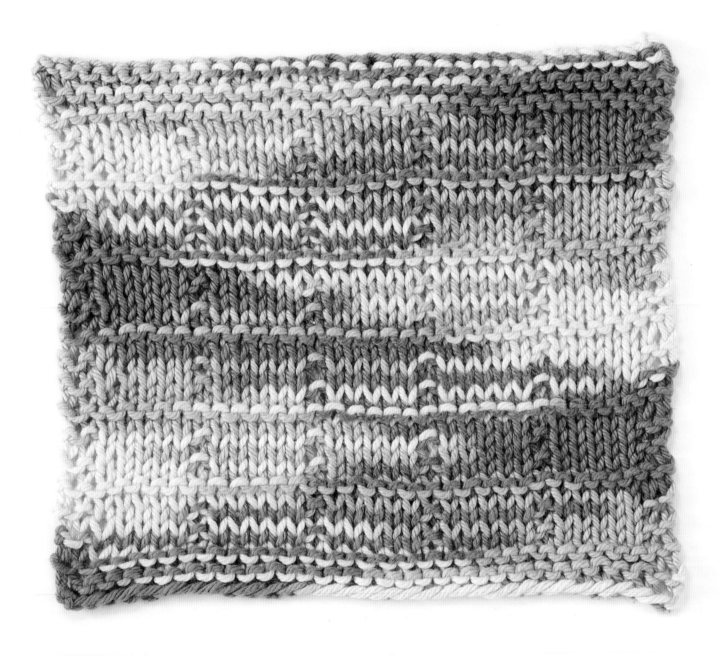

TIPTOE
by Joyce Fassbender

Perfect for both solid and multi-colored yarns, this square cloth has a simple textured pattern, using only knit and purl stitches. It's an easy, comforting project that both beginner and expert knitters will enjoy!

FINISHED MEASUREMENTS
7.5" square

YARN
Dishie™ Multi (worsted weight, 100% Cotton; 190 yards/100g): Twilight 27329, 1 skein

NEEDLES
US 7 (4.5mm) straight or circular needles

NOTIONS
Yarn Needle

GAUGE
18 sts and 24 rows = 4" in Stockinette Stitch

DIRECTIONS
Using a Long Tail Cast On, CO 33 sts.
Setup Rows: Knit three rows.

Row 1: K across.
Row 2: K1, (K1, P5) five times, K2.
Row 3: K across.
Row 4: K1, (K1, P5) five times, K2.
Row 5: K across.
Row 6: K across.
Rep Rows 1–6 five more times.

Ending Rows: Knit three rows.
BO all sts.

Finishing
Weave in ends, wash, and block.

PEBBLY
by Ann Weaver

This fun and unique project is knit using two contrasting colors and a soothing slip stitch pattern to create a useful and beautiful addition to any kitchen.

This dishcloth is worked flat, with the main stitch pattern worked first. Once complete, the Garter Stitch border is created by picking up stitches along each side and the cast on edge.

FINISHED MEASUREMENTS
8" square

YARN
Dishie™ (worsted weight, 100% Cotton; 190 yards/100g): MC Kenai 25788, CC Coffee 25399, 1 skein each

NEEDLES
US 7 (4.5mm) straight or circular needles

NOTIONS
Yarn Needle

GAUGE
20 sts and 40 rows = 4" in Garter Stitch, blocked

DIRECTIONS

Center Square
Using a Long Tail Cast On and MC, CO 35 sts.

Join CC and begin working Pebble Pattern as follows.
Row 1 (RS): With CC, (K1, Sl1 WYIB) to last st, K1.
Row 2 (WS): With CC, (K1, bring yarn to front of work, Sl1 WYIF, bring yarn to back of work) to last st, K1.
Rows 3-4: With MC, K across.
Row 5: With CC, K2, (Sl1 WYIB, K1) to last st, K1.
Row 6: With CC, K2, (bring yarn to front of work, Sl1 WYIF, bring yarn to back of work, K1) to last st, K1.
Rows 7-8: With MC, K across.
Rep Rows 1–8 seven times—eight reps of 8-row Pebble Pattern total.

WIth CC, knit two rows. Break CC.
With MC, knit two rows.
BO using MC, leaving last st live on needle.

Left Edge
Rotate work 90 degrees and PU and K 33 sts evenly spaced along edge of Center Square. 34 sts on needle.

WIth MC, knit one row.
Join CC. With CC, knit two rows. Break CC.
With MC, knit two rows.
BO using MC, leaving last st live on needle.

Bottom Edge
Rotate work 90 degrees and PU and K 33 sts evenly spaced along edge. 34 sts on needle.

With MC, knit one row.
Join CC. With CC, knit two rows. Break CC.
Using MC, knit two rows.
BO using MC, leaving last st live on needle.

Right Edge
Rotate work 90 degrees and PU and K 37 sts evenly along edge. 38 sts on needle.

Using MC, knit one row.
Join CC. Using CC, knit two rows. Break CC.
Using MC, knit two rows.
BO using MC.

Finishing
Weave in ends, wash, and enjoy!

WAVELENGTH
by Jenny Williams

Seed Stitch, Reverse Stockinette, and twisted stitches create a wavy effect. A contrasting color of Dishie Multi is worked around the edge in blanket stitch for a fun pop!

FINISHED MEASUREMENTS
10" × 10"

YARN
Dishie™ (worsted weight, 100% Cotton; 190 yards/100g);
MC Azure 25412, CC Sunshine Multi 27341, 1 skein each

NEEDLES
US 6 (4.0mm) circular or straight needles

NOTIONS
Yarn Needle

GAUGE
19 sts and 28 rows = 4" in Wavelength Chart, blocked

DIRECTIONS

With MC, CO 48 sts.

Work Wavelength Chart Sts 1–9 once, Sts 10–21 three times, and Sts 22–24 once.
Cont in established pattern through Row 24 three times.

BO all sts.

Finishing
Weave in ends.
Using CC and yarn needle, work Blanket Stitch around entire outer edge.
Wash.

LEGEND

K
RS: Knit stitch
WS: Purl stitch

P
RS: Purl stitch
WS: Knit stitch

Right Twist (RT)
Sl1 to CN, hold in back; K1, K1 from CN

Left Twist (LT)
Sl1 to CN, hold in front; K1, K1 from CN

Right Twist, Purl back (RPT)
Sl1 to CN, hold in back; K1, P1 from CN

Left Twist, Purl back (LPT)
Sl1 to CN, hold in front; P1, K1 from CN

Pattern Repeat

Wavelength Chart

RIDGED FEATHER
by Faith Schmidt

The Ridged Feather dishcloth is a fun and quick knit. The lace pattern is easy to knit and highlights the Dishie Multi yarn. The purl bumps give the cloth a nubby texture, perfect for cleaning, and it can easily be resized to fit your needs (notes are included).

FINISHED MEASUREMENTS
8.5" × 8", unblocked

YARN
Dishie™ Multi (worsted weight, 100% Cotton; 190 yards/100g): Aquarium 27340, 1 skein

NEEDLES
US 7 (4.5 mm) straight or circular needles

NOTIONS
Yarn Needle

GAUGE
18.5 sts = 4" in Ridged Feather Pattern, unblocked

To Resize: Cast on a multiple of 11 stitches plus 4, and knit to desired length.

Ridged Feather Pattern (flat over a multiple of 11 sts plus 4)
Row 1 (RS): K across.
Row 2 (WS): K2, P to last 2 sts, K2.
Row 3: K2, *(P2tog) two times, (YO, K1) three times, YO, (P2tog) two times; rep from * to last 2 sts, K2.
Row 4: K2, P to last 2 sts, K2.
Rep Rows 1–4 for pattern.

DIRECTIONS

CO 37 sts, using a Long Tail Cast On.
Knit one row.

Work Ridged Feather Pattern (Rows 1–4) 13 times.

Knit two rows.
BO P-wise.

Finishing
Weave in ends. Block, if desired.

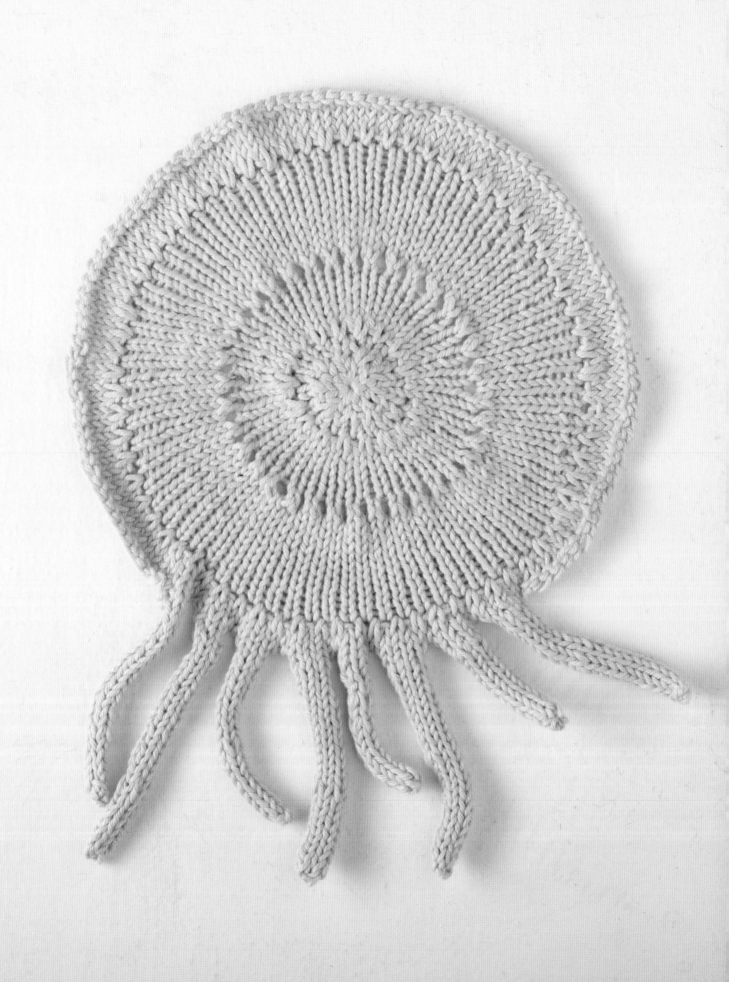

OCTOPUS
by Ann Weaver

Washing dishes has never been so fun! The Octopus dishcloth is worked in the round from the center out with tentacles created with i-cords of varying lengths. Knit up a bunch for a cephalopod party every night!

FINISHED MEASUREMENTS
10", including tentacles, blocked

YARN
Dishie™ (worsted weight, 100% Cotton; 190 yards/100g): Mint 27041, 1 skein

NEEDLES
US 7 (4.5mm) set of 4 DPNs and 16" circular needles

NOTIONS
Yarn Needle
Stitch Marker

GAUGE
18 sts and 34 rnds = 4" in Stockinette Stitch in the round, blocked

Circular Cast On
Find a photo tutorial for this cast on method here: tutorials.knitpicks.com/wptutorials/circular-cast-on.

DIRECTIONS
Using the Circular Cast On and DPNs, CO 9 sts. Arrange the sts on three DPNs so there are 3 sts on each DPN. PM for BOR.

Inc Rnd: (KFB) around. 18 sts.

Section 1
Knit three rnds.
Inc Rnd: (KFB) around. 36 sts.

Section 2
Knit seven rnds.
Inc Rnd: (K1, YO) around. 72 sts.

At this point, you will likely be able to transfer sts from DPNs to 16" circular needles.

Section 3
Knit 15 rnds.
Inc Rnd: (KFB) around. 144 sts.

Section 4
Knit three rnds.
BO Partial Rnd: BO 104 sts loosely. 40 sts remain on needle.

Tentacles
You will work 8 I-cord tentacles of 5 sts each as follows.

Using DPN, K next 5 sts from circular needle.
Slide these sts to other end of DPN.
Without turning DPN, pull yarn behind these sts tightly and knit them using a second DPN.

Cont to work I-cord until tentacle measures approx 4". Break yarn, draw through sts, and pull tight.

Rejoin yarn and K next 5 sts from circular needle. Work as for previous tentacle, working until tentacle measures approx 5".

Work six more tentacles, breaking and rejoining yarn for each tentacle, varying tentacle length as follows.
Tentacle 1: 4"
Tentacle 2: 5"
Tentacle 3: 3"
Tentacle 4: 4"
Tentacle 5: 2.5"
Tentacle 6: 3.5"
Tentacle 7: 2"
Tentacle 8: 3"

Finishing
Weave in ends, wash, and enjoy!

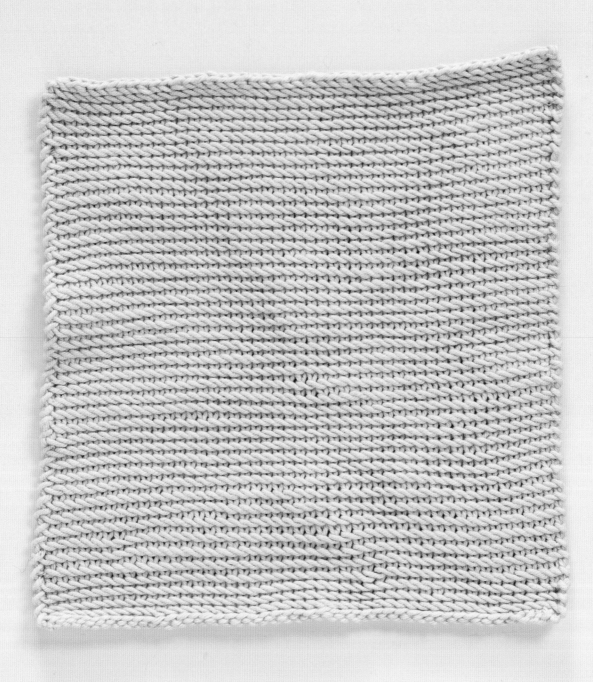

HORIZONTAL WRAPPED STITCH
by Jenny Williams

For anyone looking for a dishcloth with heavy scrubbing power, you can't go wrong with this project. The Horizontal Wrapped Stitch dishcloth features an easy to memorize stitch pattern that creates a dense fabric that is completely reversible.

FINISHED MEASUREMENTS
9" square

YARN
Dishie™ (worsted weight, 100% Cotton; 190 yards/100g): Mint 27041, 1 skein

NEEDLES
US 5 (3.75mm) circular or straight needles

NOTIONS
Yarn Needle

GAUGE
22 sts and 39 rows = 4" in stitch pattern, washed and blocked

Pattern Notes
Keep the wraps fairly loose, but even. Take care not to lose the yarn over of Row 1 when turning for Row 2. When working Row 2, each yarn over should cross over in front of the slipped stitch—insert the right-hand needle through the back of both the yarn over and the stitch to knit them together.

K2tog TBL decreases are always worked with yarn over loop and slipped stitch knit together.

DIRECTIONS
CO 47 sts.

Row 1 (WS): (Sl1 K-wise, YO) to end.
Row 2 (RS): (K2tog TBL) to end.
Rep Rows 1–2 for 9".

BO all sts.

Finishing
Weave in ends. Wash and block; stretch out and pin to make it look especially neat.

SOMETHING FISHY
by Stana D. Sortor

A fish-shaped washcloth is sure to bring lot of giggles to every bath time, or it might even bring some helpers for cleaning chores around the house.

This project is knit in Garter Stitch, starting at the mouth towards the tail, with increases and decreases worked on either end. The last stitch of every row is slipped purl-wise with yarn in front for a nice edge.

Make a two-color striped fish, or choose to omit the directions for MC/CC stripes and make a single-color fish. When working stripes, twist the non-working yarn around the working yarn along the edge.

Embroider the eye with a small piece of black yarn.

An optional step is to create a small fold for hanging the fish, or catching it on a hook, by folding the cast on edge to the wrong side approx 0.5" in, then sew the edge to the wrong side of the fish.

FINISHED MEASUREMENTS
8" width × 14" length (from mouth to tail)

YARN
Dishie™ (worsted weight, 100% Cotton; 190 yards/100g):
MC Swan 25409, CC Beach Front Multi 27332, 1 skein each

NEEDLES
US 7 (4.5mm) straight or circular needles

NOTIONS
Yarn Needle
Stitch Markers
Small Amount of Black Yarn (worsted weight)

GAUGE
18 sts and 28 rows = 4" in Garter Stitch, blocked

DIRECTIONS

Body
With MC, CO 8 sts.
Rows 1-2: K7, Sl1.
Row 3: K1, KFB, K4, KFB, Sl1. 10 sts.
Row 4: K9, Sl1.
Row 5: K1, KFB, K6, KFB, Sl1. 12 sts.
Row 6: K11, Sl1.
Row 7: K1, KFB, K8, KFB, Sl1. 14 sts.
Row 8: K13, Sl1.
Row 9: K1, KFB, K10, KFB, Sl1. 16 sts.
Row 10: K15, Sl1.
Row 11: K1, KFB, K12, KFB, Sl1. 18 sts.
Row 12: K17, Sl1.
Row 13: K1, KFB, K14, KFB, Sl1. 20 sts.
Row 14: K19, Sl1.
Row 15: K1, KFB, K16, KFB, Sl1. 22 sts.
Row 16: K21, Sl1.
Row 17: K1, KFB, K18, KFB, Sl1. 24 sts.
Row 18: K23, Sl1.
Row 19: K1, KFB, K20, KFB, Sl1. 26 sts.
Rows 20-22: K25, Sl1.
Row 23: K1, KFB, K22, KFB, Sl1. 28 sts.
Row 24: K27, Sl1.
Row 25: K1, KFB, K24, KFB, Sl1. 30 sts.
Row 26: K29, Sl1.

Join CC.
Rows 27-28: With CC, K29, Sl1.
Row 29: With CC, K1, KFB, K26, KFB, Sl1. 32 sts.
Row 30: With CC, K31, Sl1.
Row 31: With MC, K1, KFB, K28, KFB, Sl1. 34 sts.
Rows 32-34: With MC, K33, Sl1.
Row 35: With CC, K1, KFB, K30, KFB, Sl1. 36 sts.
Rows 36-38: With CC, K35, Sl1.
Rows 39-40: With MC, K35, Sl1.
Row 41: With MC, K1, SSK, K30, K2tog, Sl1. 34 sts.
Row 42: With MC, K33, Sl1.
Rows 43-44: With CC, K33, Sl1.
Row 45: With CC, K1, SSK, K28, K2tog, Sl1. 32 sts.
Row 46: With CC, K31, Sl1.
Rows 47-48: With MC, K31, Sl1.
Row 49: With MC, K1, SSK, K26, K2tog, Sl1. 30 sts.
Row 50: With MC, K29, Sl1.
Row 51: With CC, K1, SSK, K24, K2tog, Sl1. 28 sts.
Rows 52-54: With CC, K27, Sl1.
Row 55: With MC, K1, SSK, K22, K2tog, Sl1. 26 sts.
Row 56: With MC, K25, Sl1.
Row 57: With MC, K1, SSK, K20, K2tog, Sl1. 24 sts.
Row 58: With MC, K23, Sl1.
Rows 59-60: With CC, K23, Sl1.
Row 61: With CC, K1, SSK, K18, K2tog, Sl1. 22 sts.
Row 62: With CC, K21, Sl1.

Row 63: With MC, K1, SSK, K16, K2tog, Sl1. 20 sts.

Rows 64–66: With MC, K19, Sl1.

Row 67: With CC, K1, SSK, K14, K2tog, Sl1. 18 sts.

Row 68: With CC, K17, Sl1.

Row 69: With CC, K1, SSK, K12, K2tog, Sl1. 16 sts.

Row 70: With CC, K15, Sl1.

Rows 71–72: With MC, K15, Sl1.

Row 73: With MC, K1, SSK, K10, K2tog, Sl1. 14 sts.

Row 74: With MC, K13, Sl1.

Row 75: With CC, K1, SSK, K8, K2tog, Sl1. 12 sts.

Rows 76–78: With CC, K11, Sl1.

Row 79: With MC, K1, SSK, K6, K2tog, Sl1. 10 sts.

Row 80: With MC, K9, Sl1.

Row 81: With MC, K1, SSK, K4, K2tog, Sl1. 8 sts.

Row 82: With MC, K7, Sl1.

Break MC. Cont with CC only.

Row 83: K1, SSK, K2, K2tog, Sl1. 6 sts.

Row 84: K5, Sl1.

Row 85: K1, SSK, K2tog, Sl1. 4 sts.

Row 86: K3, Sl1.

Tail

Row 87: K1, (KFB) two times, Sl1. 6 sts.

Row 88: (P1, K1) two times, P1, Sl1.

Row 89: K1, KFB, P1, K1, KFB, Sl1. 8 sts.

Row 90: (K1, P1) three times, K1, Sl1.

Row 91: K1, KFB, (K1, P1) two times, KFB, Sl1. 10 sts.

Row 92: (P1, K1) four times, P1, Sl1.

Row 93: K1, KFB, (P1, K1) three times, KFB, Sl1. 12 sts.

Row 94: (K1, P1) five times, K1, Sl1.

Row 95: K1, KFB, (K1, P1) four times, KFB, Sl1. 14 sts.

Row 96: (P1, K1) six times, P1, Sl1.

Row 97: K1, KFB, (P1, K1) five times, KFB, Sl1. 16 sts.

Row 98: (K1, P1) seven times, K1, Sl1.

Row 99: K1, KFB, (K1, P1) six times, KFB, Sl1. 18 sts.

Row 100: (P1, K1) eight times, P1, Sl1.

Row 101: K1, KFB, (P1, K1) seven times, KFB, Sl1. 20 sts.

Row 102: (K1, P1) nine times, K1, Sl1.

BO in (K1, P1) pattern.

Finishing

To create a small fold for hanging fish, fold CO edge to WS approx 0.5" from CO edge, then sew edge to WS of fish.

Embroider eye onto fish face.

Weave in ends, wash, and block to measurements.

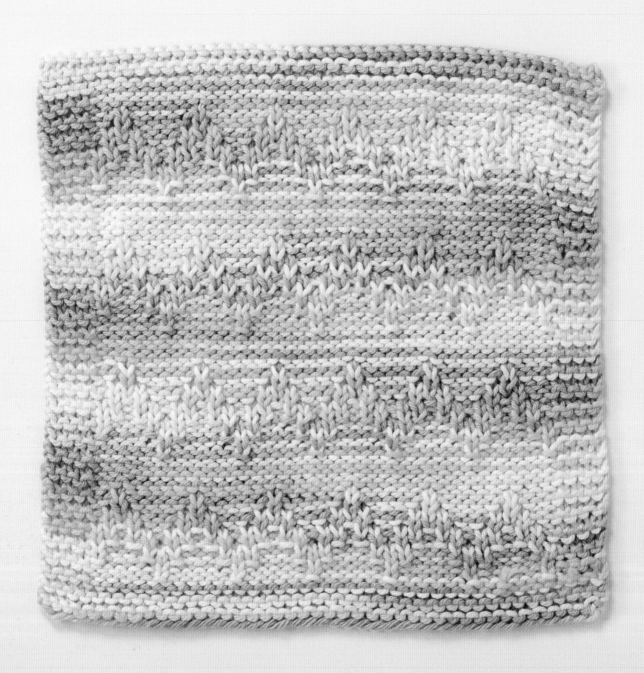

HEARTBEAT
by Knit Picks Design Team

This dishcloth is perfect for anyone looking for a fun, quick project. Knit in a simple chevron pattern, the dishcloth is bordered by Garter Stitch to keep it nice and flat. Work one up for a charming addition to any kitchen.

FINISHED MEASUREMENTS
8.5" square

YARN
Dishie™ Multi (worsted weight, 100% Cotton; 190 yards/100g): Sailboat 28084, 1 skein

NEEDLES
US 7 (4.5 mm) straight or circular needles

NOTIONS
Yarn Needle
Stitch Markers

GAUGE
20 sts and 28 rows = 4" in Heartbeat Pattern, blocked

Heartbeat Pattern (flat over a multiple of 6 sts plus 6)
Row 1 (WS): K across.
Row 2 (RS): P across.
Rows 3: (K5, P1) to end.
Rows 4: (K1, P5) to end.
Rows 5: P1, (K3, P3) to last 5 sts. K3, P2.
Rows 6: K2, (P3, K3) to last 4 sts. P3, K1.
Rows 7: (P2, K1) to end.
Rows 8: (P1, K2) to end.
Rows 9: K1, (P3, K3) to last 5 sts. P3, K2.
Rows 10: P2, (K3, P3) to last 4 sts. K3, P1.
Rows 11: K2, (P1, K5) to last 4 sts P1, K3.
Rows 12: P3 (K1, P5) to last 3 sts, K1, P2.
Row 13: K across.
Row 14: P across.
Rep Rows 1–14 for pattern.

DIRECTIONS
Loosely CO 44 sts.
Knit four rows.

Row 1: K4, work Row 1 of Heartbeat Pattern to last 4 sts, K4.
Row 2: K4, work Row 2 of Heartbeat Pattern to last 4 sts, K4.
Work as established, working through Heartbeat Pattern, with 4 K sts at each end. Work until piece measures 8" from CO edge, approx four reps total, ending after a Row 14.

Knit four rows.
BO all sts.

Finishing
Weave in ends, wash, and block if desired.

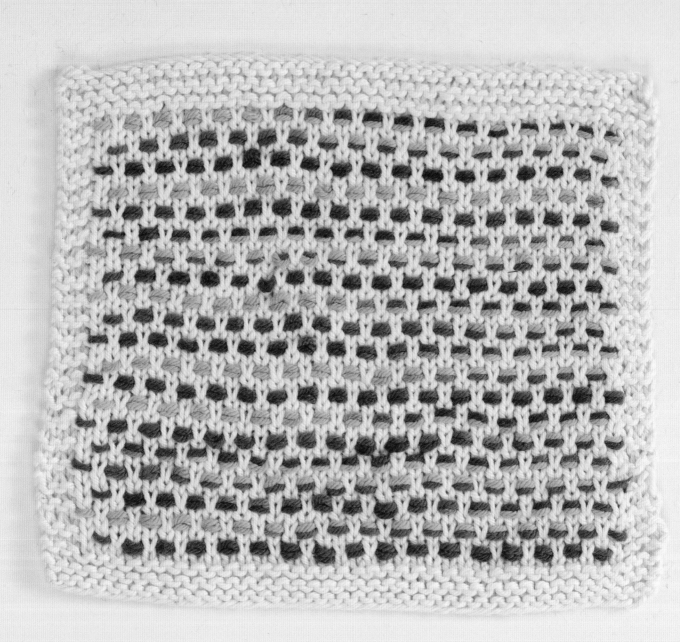

WOVEN POLKA DOTS
by Emily Ringelman

This simple dishcloth is ideal for knitters who like the look of colorwork, but dislike knitting it. The contrast color is never knitted; it is woven through Slipped stitches of the main color. This is an ideal use of a highly variegated yarn because pooling will never happen within such small dots.

FINISHED MEASUREMENTS
8" square

YARN
Dishie™ (worsted weight, 100% Cotton; 190 yards/100g):
MC Swan 25409, CC Caterpillar Multi 27342, 1 skein each

NEEDLES
US 7 (4.5mm) straight or circular needles

NOTIONS
Yarn Needle

GAUGE
20 sts and 24 rows = 4" in Slip Stitch Polka Dot pattern, blocked

Note that all stitches are slipped P-wise.

Slip Stitch Polka Dot (flat over an odd number of sts)
Row 1 (RS): With MC, K across.
Row 2 (WS): With MC, K3, P to last 3, K3.
Row 3: Sl4, (with CC, Sl1 WYIF, Sl1 WYIB) to last 5 sts, Sl1 WYIF, drop yarn to back of work, Sl4.
Row 4: Sl6, bring CC across front of last 2 sts, (Sl1 WYIB, Sl1 WYIF) to last 5 sts, Sl1 WYIB, drop yarn to front, Sl4.
Row 5: With MC, K across.
Row 6: With MC, K3, P to last 3, K3.
Row 7: Sl3, (with CC, Sl1 WYIF, Sl1 WYIB) to last 4 sts, Sl1 WYIF, drop yarn to back, Sl3.
Row 8: Sl5, bring CC across front of last 2 sts, (Sl1 WYIB, Sl1 WYIF) to last 4 sts, Sl1 WFIB, drop yarn to front, Sl3.
Rep Rows 1–8 for pattern.

DIRECTIONS
With MC, CO 41 sts.
Knit five rows.

Work Slip Stitch Polka Dot pattern.
Rep the 8 rows of Slip Stitch Polka Dot until piece measures 7.5" from CO edge, ending after a RS row.

With MC, knit five rows.
BO K-wise.

Finishing
Weave in ends, wash, and block as you like.

XYLOCO
by Joyce Fassbender

Nupps (or bobbles) can be intimidating in lace knitting if you've never come across them before. Get a little practice on this lovely dishcloth—and have a useful addition to the kitchen! This dishcloth is great for both solid and multi-colored yarns and features only knit and purl stitches, in addition to the nupps.

FINISHED MEASUREMENTS
8″ square

YARN
Dishie™ Multi (worsted weight, 100% Cotton; 190 yards/100g): Caterpillar 27342, 1 skein

NEEDLES
US 7 (4.5mm) straight or circular needles

NOTIONS
Yarn Needle

GAUGE
18 sts and 24 rows = 4″ in Stockinette Stitch

Nupp
On RS, loosely work (K1, YO, K1, YO, K1) into same stitch, turn work, P5tog, turn work, slip stitch.

DIRECTIONS
CO 36 sts using a Long Tail Cast On.

Row 1 (WS): (K3, P3) six times.
Row 2 (RS): (K3, P1, nupp, p1) six times.
Row 3: (K3, P3) six times.
Row 4: (P3, K3) six times.
Row 5: (P3, K1, nupp, K1) six times.
Row 6: (P3, K3) six times.
Rep Rows 1–6 six times.
Rep Rows 1–3 once more.

BO all sts.

Finishing
Weave in ends, wash, and block.

CRYPTODIRA
by Knit Picks Design Team

Reptile lovers rejoice! Cryptodira is a suborder that includes most tortoises and turtles and the wrapped stitches in this pattern evoke their skin. While the original is worked up in a multi-colored yarn, this pattern is also wonderful in solid-colored yarn.

FINISHED MEASUREMENTS
8.5" square

YARN
Dishie™ Multi (worsted weight, 100% Cotton; 190 yards/100g): Sea Turtle 28092, 1 skein

NEEDLES
US 7 (4.5 mm) straight or circular needles

NOTIONS
Yarn Needle
Stitch Markers

GAUGE
20 sts and 28 rows = 4" in Wrapped Stitch Pattern, blocked

Wrapped Stich Pattern (flat over a multiple of 4 sts plus 1)
Row 1 (RS): (K2, Sl2 WYIF, bring yarn to back, Sl sts back to RH needle, K these 2 sts) to last 5 sts, K5.
Row 2 (WS): P all.
Row 3: K4, (Sl2 WYIF, bring yarn to back, Sl sts back to RH needle, K these 2 sts, K2) to last st, K1.
Row 4: P all.
Rep Rows 1–4 for pattern.

DIRECTIONS
Loosely CO 45 sts.
Knit four rows.
Purl one row.

Row 1 (RS): K4, work Row 1 of Wrapped Stitch Pattern to last 4 sts, K4.
Row 2: K4, work Row 2 of Wrapped Stitch Pattern to last 4 sts, K4.
Cont as established, working through Wrapped Stitch Pattern, with 4 K sts at each end, until piece measures 8" from beginning, ending after a stitch pattern Row 4.

Knit four rows.
BO all sts.

Finishing
Weave in ends, wash, and block if desired.

SASA
by Joyce Fassbender

Named for a type of bamboo, this highly textured dishcloth uses only knits and purls to create a beautiful and fun pattern. The easy-to-knit project has a textured pattern that makes for a great surface for washing.

FINISHED MEASUREMENTS
7.25" square

YARN
CotLin™ (DK weight, 70% Tanguis Cotton, 30% Linen; 123 yards/50g): Lichen 26674, 1 skein

NEEDLES
US 6 (4mm) straight or circular needles

NOTIONS
Yarn Needle

GAUGE
24 sts and 28 rows = 4" in Stockinette Stitch

DIRECTIONS
CO 44 sts using a Long Tail Cast On.
Knit three rows.

Row 1: K2, (P2, K4, P2) five times, K2.
Row 2: K2, (K2, P4, K2) five times, K2.
Row 3: K2, (P2, K4, P2) five times, K2.
Row 4: K2, (P2, K1, P2, K1, P2) five times, K2.
Row 5: K2, (K3, P2, K3) five times, K2.
Row 6: K2, (P2, K1, P2, K1, P2) five times, K2.
Rep Rows 1–6 seven more times.
Rep Rows 1–3 once more.

Knit three rows.
BO all sts.

Finishing
Weave in ends, wash, and block.

MARLED COLORSHIFT
by Ann Weaver

Play with color with this fun, oversized dishcloth. The marled look is created by holding two different colors of yarn together and using simple Stockinette Stitch. Each project is unique and is a wonderful way to explore color shifting projects. Choose shades of the same color for a gradient look or try contrasting colors—either way this easy project is perfect for beginners and advanced knitters alike.

FINISHED MEASUREMENTS
10″ × 11″

YARN
Dishie™ (worsted weight, 100% Cotton; 190 yards/100g):
C1 Coffee 25399, C2 Honeydew 25410, C3 Crème Brûlée 25404, C4 Clarity 27037, 1 skein each

NEEDLES
US 10 (6mm) straight or circular needles

NOTIONS
Yarn Needle
2 Stitch Markers

GAUGE
14 sts and 22 rows = 4″ in Stockinette Stitch with yarn held double, blocked

DIRECTIONS

With C1 and C2 held tog, CO 2 sts, PM, CO 30 sts, PM, CO 2 sts. 34 sts total.
Knit three rows.

Row 1 (RS): K across.
Row 2 (WS): K2, SM, P to second M, SM, K2.
Work Rows 1–2 a total of nine times, 18 rows total.

Break C1 and join C3.
With C2 and C3 held tog, work Rows 1–2 a total of nine times, 18 rows total.

Break C2 and join C4.
With C3 and C4 held tog, work Rows 1–2 a total of nine times, 18 rows total.

Knit three rows.
BO all sts.

Finishing
Weave in ends, wash, and enjoy!

LITTLE LEAF
by Jenny Williams

Sweet little leaves dance across this dishcloth, creating a fun and functional project. An I-Cord Bind Off keeps the edges tidy.

FINISHED MEASUREMENTS
9″ × 8.5″

YARN
Dishie™ (worsted weight, 100% Cotton; 190 yards/100g); MC Honeydew 25410, CC Jalapeño 25785, 1 skein each

NEEDLES
US 5 (3.75mm) circular or straight needles

NOTIONS
Yarn Needle

GAUGE
19 sts and 30 rows = 4″ in Little Leaf Chart, blocked

Chart Note
Work Rows 1-6 of Leaf Chart in the blue outlined sections of Little Leaf Chart.

DIRECTIONS
Using MC, CO 37 sts.

Row 1 (RS): Work Little Leaf Chart Sts 1-3 once, work boxed rep Sts 4-9 five times, work Sts 10-13 once. Cont in established pattern through Row 24 of Little Leaf Chart twice.
Work chart Rows 1-12 once more.

I-Cord Bind Off
Drop MC. Using CC, CO 3 additional sts to LH needle.
Step 1: K2, K2tog.
Step 2: Sl3 sts from RH needle to LH.
Rep Steps 1-2 (in CC) across all sts.
Using LH needle, PU and K 1 st at corner. Rep Steps 1-2.
Using LH needle, PU and K 1 st along left edge of dishcloth.
Rep Steps 1-2. Cont in established BO around all four edges.
Break yarn and weave end into first BO sts.

Finishing
Weave in remaining ends and wash.

Little Leaf Chart

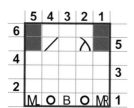

Leaf Chart

LEGEND

No Stitch
Placeholder—no stitch made

K
RS: Knit stitch
WS: Purl stitch

P
RS: Purl stitch
WS: Knit stitch

K TBL
RS: Knit stitch through the back loop
WS: Purl stitch through the back loop

YO
Yarn over

M1R
Make 1 right-leaning stitch

M1L
Make 1 left-leaning stitch

K2tog
Knit 2 stitches together as one stitch

SKP
Slip 1 knit-wise, knit 1, pass slip stitch over knit stitch

CDD
Slip first and second stitches together as if to K2tog; knit 1 stitch; pass 2 slipped stitches over the knit stitch

Work Rows 1-6 of Leaf Chart

Pattern Repeat

CANDLEBERRY
by Joyce Fassbender

A unique construction and plenty of lace techniques make the Candleberry dishcloth a favorite quick-but-interesting project. Worked in the round from the inside out, the pattern includes yarn overs and decreases, with a few nupps scattered throughout. A fun project as well as a beautiful addition to your kitchen.

FINISHED MEASUREMENTS
8.5" square

YARN
Shine™ (sport weight, 60% Pima Cotton, 40% Modal; 110 yards/50g): Peapod 25342, 1 skein

NEEDLES
US 5 (3.75mm) DPNs

NOTIONS
Yarn Needle

GAUGE
22 sts and 30 rnds = 4" in Stockinette Stitch in the round

Chart Notes
The chart is worked in the round; read each chart row from right to left as a RS row.
Only odd numbered rows are charted; work all even numbered rows as: K all sts.

Circular Cast On
Find a photo tutorial for this cast on method here:
tutorials.knitpicks.com/wptutorials/circular-cast-on.

DIRECTIONS
CO 8 sts using the Circular Cast On.
Knit one rnd.

Rnd 1: (Work Row 1 of Candleberry Chart, K1) four times.
Rnd 2: K all.
Cont as established through Row 29 of chart.

Knit one rnd.
BO all sts.

Finishing
Weave in ends, wash, and block.

LEGEND

■	**No Stitch** Placeholder—no stitch made		
□	**Knit Stitch**	○	**YO** Yarn over
╱	**K2tog** Knit 2 stitches together as one stitch		
╲	**SSK** Slip, slip, knit slipped stitches together		
⟋	**K3tog** Knit 3 stitches together as one stitch		
⋏	**SK2P** Slip 1 knit-wise, K2tog, pass slip stitch over K2tog		
⬚	**Nupp** Into next stitch: K1, YO, K1, YO, K1; turn work, Purl 5 together		

Candleberry Chart

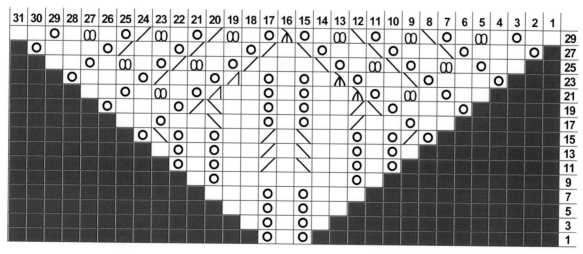

WAVY RIB
by Faith Schmidt

Wavy Rib Dishcloth is a fun and quick knit. The stitch pattern is easy to memorize, and becomes intuitive after a few repeats. While both sides are not identical, the wrong side has a great look too. It can easily be resized to fit your needs.

FINISHED MEASUREMENTS
8.5″ × 9.5″, lightly blocked

YARN
Dishie™ (worsted weight, 100% Cotton; 190 yards/100g): Jalapeño 25785, 1 skein

NEEDLES
US 4 (3.5 mm) straight or circular needles

NOTIONS
Yarn Needle

GAUGE
26 sts = 4″ in Wavy Rib Pattern, unblocked and unstretched

Pattern Notes
This dishcloth is knit at a tighter-than-usual gauge to allow the rib stitches to pop. Knitting at a looser gauge may affect the look of the finished piece.

When the instructions state, "K the knits and P the purls", this means to knit whatever stitch you are seeing on the needle. So, if the next stitch looks like a knit stitch, you will knit it; if it looks like a purl, you will purl it.

To Resize: Cast on a multiple of 6 stitches, plus 2, and work to desired length.

Wavy Rib Pattern (flat over a multiple of 6 sts plus 2)
Row 1 (RS): (P2, K4) to last 2 sts, P2.
Row 2 (WS): K the knits and P the purls.
Rows 3–6: Rep Rows 1-2 two more times.
Row 7: (K3, P2, K1) to last 2 sts, K2.
Row 8: K the knits and P the purls.
Rows 9–12: Rep Rows 7-8 two more times.

DIRECTIONS
CO 50 sts, using a Long Tail Cast On.

Work Wavy Rib Pattern (Rows 1–12) five times. Rep pattern Rows 1–5 once more.

BO K-wise.

Finishing
Weave in ends. Block lightly, if desired.

Wavy Rib Pattern

	8	7	6	5	4	3	2	1	
12				●	●				
				●	●				11
10				●	●				
				●	●				9
8				●	●				
				●	●				7
6	●	●					●	●	
	●	●					●	●	5
4	●	●					●	●	
	●	●					●	●	3
2	●	●					●	●	
	●	●					●	●	1

LEGEND

K
RS: Knit stitch
WS: Purl stitch

● P
RS: Purl stitch
WS: Knit stitch

☐ Pattern Repeat

WELTED LEAF
by Faith Schmidt

The Welted Leaf dishcloth is full of texture and is a quick and fun knit. Knit completely in knits and purls, it's a perfect pattern for beginner knitters or a mindless project for an expert. Need a bigger or smaller size? Instructions are included on how to resize to fit your needs.

FINISHED MEASUREMENTS
8.5″ × 9″, unblocked

YARN
Dishie™ (worsted weight, 100% Cotton; 190 yards/100g): Jalapeño 25785, 1 skein

NEEDLES
US 5 (4.5mm) straight or circular needles

NOTIONS
Yarn Needle

GAUGE
21 sts = 4″ in Welted Leaf Stitch, unblocked

This stitch pattern shows up better with a tighter gauge than you might normally use.

To Resize: Cast on a multiple of 8 stitches plus 4, and work to desired length.

Welted Leaf Stitch (flat over a multiple of 8 sts plus 4)
Row 1 (RS): K across.
Row 2 (WS): K2, P to last 2 sts, K2.
Row 3: K2, (K4, P4) to last 2 sts, K2.
Row 4: K5, (P4, K4) to last 7 sts, P4, K3.
Row 5: K2, P2, (K4, P4) to last 8 sts, K4, P2, K2.
Row 6: K3, (P4, K4) to last 9 sts, P4, K5.
Row 7: K5, (P4, K4) to last 7 sts, P4, K3.
Row 8: K2, P2, (K4, P4) to last 8 sts, K4, P2, K2.
Row 9: K3, (P4, K4) to last 9 sts, P4, K5.
Row 10: K2, (P4, K4) to last 2 sts, K2.
Rep Rows 1–10 for pattern.

DIRECTIONS

CO 44 sts, using a Long Tail Cast On.
Knit one row.

Work Welted Leaf Stitch (Rows 1–10) seven times total.
Work Rows 1–2 once more.

Next Row (RS): K2, P to last 2 sts, K2.
BO all sts P-wise.

Finishing
Weave in ends. Block if desired.

RINTHE
by Joyce Fassbender

A reversible square cloth worked from the bottom up, the Rinthe dishcloth is a fast and fun project for knitters of all levels. Simple knits and purls create a raised labyrinth design, and the Dishie yarn means this dishcloth will last wash after wash.

FINISHED MEASUREMENTS

8.5" square

YARN

Dishie™ (worsted weight, 100% Cotton; 190 yards/100g): Douglas Fir 27036, 1 skein

NEEDLES

US 7 (4.5mm) straight or circular needles

NOTIONS

Yarn Needle

GAUGE

18 sts and 24 rows = 4" in Stockinette Stitch

DIRECTIONS

CO 40 sts using a Long Tail Cast On.

Rows 1–2: P40.

Rows 3–4: K40.

Row 5: P40.

Row 6: K2, P36, K2.

Row 7: P2, K36, P2.

Row 8: K2, P2, K32, P2, K2.

Row 9: P2, K2, P32, K2, P2.

Row 10: K2, P2, K2, P28, K2, P2, K2.

Row 11: P2, K2, P2, K28, P2, K2, P2.

Row 12: (K2, P2) two times, K24, (P2, K2) two times.

Row 13: (P2, K2) two times, P24, (K2, P2) two times.

Row 14: (K2, P2) two times, K2, P20, (K2, P2) two times, K2.

Row 15: P2, (K2, P2) two times, K20, P2, (K2, P2) two times.

Row 16: (K2, P2) three times, K16, (P2, K2) three times.

Row 17: (P2, K2) three times, P16, (K2, P2) three times.

Row 18: (K2, P2) three times, K2, P12, (K2, P2) three times, K2.

Row 19: P2, (K2, P2) three times, K12, P2, (K2, P2) three times.

Row 20: (K2, P2) four times, K8, (P2, K2) four times.

Row 21: (P2, K2) four times, P8, (K2, P2) four times.

Row 22: (K2, P2) four times, K2, P4, (K2, P2) four times, K2.

Row 23: P2, (K2, P2) four times, K4, P2, (K2, P2) four times.

Row 24: (K2, P2) four times, K4, (P2, K2) five times.

Row 25: (P2, K2) five times, P4, (K2, P2) four times.

Row 26: (K2, P2) three times, K2, P8, (K2, P2) four times, K2.

Row 27: P2, (K2, P2) four times, K8, P2, (K2, P2) three times.

Row 28: (K2, P2) three times, K12, (P2, K2) four times.

Row 29: (P2, K2) four times, P12, (K2, P2) three times.

Row 30: (K2, P2) two times, K2, P16, (K2, P2) three times, K2.

Row 31: P2, (K2, P2) three times, K16, P2, (K2, P2) two times.

Row 32: (K2, P2) two times, K20, (P2, K2) three times.

Row 33: (P2, K2) three times, P20, (K2, P2) two times.

Row 34: K2, P2, K2, P24, K2, (P2, K2) two times.

Row 35: (P2, K2) two times, P2, K24, P2, K2, P2.

Row 36: K2, P2, K28, P2, K2, P2, K2.

Row 37: P2, K2, P2, K2, P28, K2, P2.

Row 38: K2, P32, K2, P2, K2.

Row 39: P2, K2, P2, K32, P2.

Row 40: K36, P2, K2.

Row 41: P2, K2, P36.

Row 42: P38, K2.

Row 43: P2, K38.

Row 44: K40.

Rows 45–46: P40.

Rows 47–48: K40.

Row 49: P40.

BO all sts.

Finishing

Weave in ends, wash, and block.

MITERED QUARTERS
by Allison Griffith

Play with color while practicing some fun techniques! Knit completely in Garter Stitch, this dishcloth uses short rows to create a geometric design that mimics the look of mitered squares. It's a perfect project for using up those odds & ends of leftover yarn!

This dishcloth is worked flat in one piece, the wide side of the green section to the wide side of the blue section. Only on the first and last rows are all the stitches worked.

FINISHED MEASUREMENTS
7.5" square

YARN
Dishie™ (worsted weight, 100% Cotton; 190 yards/100g):
MC Jalapeño 25785, C1 Silver 25789, C2 Ash 27040,
C3 Kenai 25788, 1 skein each

NEEDLES
US 6 (4mm) straight or circular needles

NOTIONS
Yarn Needle

GAUGE
19 sts and 37 rows = 4" in Garter Stitch, lightly blocked

DIRECTIONS

First Half
With MC, CO 36 sts and work flat.
Row 1: K35, W&T.
Row 2 (and all even-numbered rows): K across.
Row 3: K34, W&T.
Row 5 (and all following odd-numbered rows): K to 2 sts before closest W&T gap, W&T.

Cont until you are working 21 sts, ending on an even-numbered row.
Break MC.

Join C1 and cont in pattern as established until you are working 2 sts, ending on an even-numbered row.
Break C1.

Second Half
Join C2.
Row 1 (and all odd-numbered rows): K to closest W&T gap, knitting wrap tog with the last st.
Row 2 (and all even-numbered rows): Sl1 K-wise, K to end.

Cont until you are working 20 sts, ending on an even-numbered row.
Break C2.

Join C3 and cont in pattern as established until you are working 36 sts, ending on an even-numbered row.
BO all 36 sts.

Finishing
Weave in ends, wash, and block to measurements.

LOG CABIN TEXTURAMA!

by Ann Weaver

With a unique mix of texture and construction, this pattern will keep you on your toes. Inspired by log cabin quilts, this dishcloth starts in the middle with a striped square of simple knit and slipped stitches. The edges are then picked up and knit to create the border. Use two colors with high contrast or go more muted with two neutrals; no matter your choice, you'll have a beautiful dishcloth in no time.

FINISHED MEASUREMENTS
8″ square

YARN
Dishie™ (worsted weight, 100% Cotton; 190 yards/100g):
MC Pomegranate 25402, CC Mint 27041, 1 skein each

NEEDLES
US 7 (4.5mm) straight or circular needles

NOTIONS
Yarn Needle

GAUGE
20 sts and 40 rows = 4″ in Garter Stitch, blocked

Texture Pattern
Row 1 (RS): With CC, (K1, Sl1 WYIB) to last st, K1.
Row 2 (WS): With CC, (K1, bring yarn to front of work, Sl1 WYIF, bring yarn to back of work) to last st, K1.
Rows 3–4: With MC, rep Rows 1–2.
Rows 5–6: With CC, K across.
Rows 7–8: With MC, rep Rows 1–2.
Rows 9–10: With CC, rep Rows 1–2.
Rows 11–12: With MC, K across.
Rep Rows 1–12 for pattern.

DIRECTIONS

Center Square
Using a Long Tail Cast On and MC, CO 21 sts.
Join CC, but do not break MC.

Work Texture patterns Rows 1–12 three times.
Break CC.

BO using MC, leaving last st live on needle.

Left Edge
Rotate work 90 degrees and PU and K 20 sts evenly spaced along edge of Center Square. 21 sts on needle.

Join CC and work Rows 1–12 of Texture Pattern across these sts once, then work Rows 1–6 once more.
Break CC.

BO using MC, leaving last st live on needle.

Bottom Edge
Rotate work 90 degrees and PU and K 32 sts evenly spaced along edge. 33 sts on needle.

Join CC, and work Rows 1–12 of Texture Pattern across these sts once, then work Rows 1–6 once more.
Break CC.

BO using MC, leaving last st live on needle.

Right Edge
Rotate work 90 degrees and PU and K 32 sts evenly spaced along edge. 33 sts on needle.

Join CC and work Rows 1–12 of Texture Pattern across these sts once, then work Rows 1–6 once more.
Break CC.

BO using MC, leaving last st live on needle.

Top Edge
Rotate work 90 degrees and PU and K 42 sts evenly spaced along edge. 43 sts on needle.

Join CC and work Rows 1–12 of Texture Pattern across these sts once, then work Rows 1–6 once more.
Break CC.

With MC, BO all sts.

Finishing
Weave in ends, wash, and enjoy!

FOOTBALL
by Emily Ringelman

This simple washcloth is worked from point to point with a thin garter stitch edging to prevent rolling. The two white stripes near the ends are worked like stripes, while the central white stripe and laces are worked in duplicate stitch after the washcloth is complete. Make several of these for your next Superbowl party!

FINISHED MEASUREMENTS
5.5" × 9.5"

YARN
Dishie™ (worsted weight, 100% Cotton; 190 yards/100g): MC Coffee 25399, CC Swan 25409, 1 skein each

NEEDLES
US 7 (4.5mm) straight or circular needles

NOTIONS
Yarn Needle

GAUGE
20 sts and 28 rows = 4" in Stockinette Stitch, blocked

DIRECTIONS
With MC, CO 3 sts.

Bottom
Row 1 (RS): KFB, K1, KFB. 5 sts.
Row 2 (WS): KFB, K to last st, KFB. 2 sts inc.
Row 3: KFB, K to last st, KFB. 2 sts inc.
Rep Rows 2-3 two more times. 17 sts.

Row 8: K2, P to last 2 sts, K2.
Row 9: KFB, K to last st, KFB. 19 sts.
Row 10: Rep Row 8.

Increase Section
Switch to CC (do not break MC, carry it behind CC) and work the following Rows 1-4 once.
Row 1 (RS): K across.
Row 2 (WS): K2, P to last 2 sts, K2.
Row 3: KFB, K to last st, KFB. 21 sts.
Row 4: Rep Row 2.
Break CC, switch to MC, and work Rows 1-4 three more times. 27 sts.

Middle
Row 1 (RS): K across.
Row 2 (WS): K2, P to last 2 sts, K2.
Rep Rows 1-2 four more times.

Decrease Section
Row 1 (RS): SSK, K to last 2 sts, K2tog. 25 sts.
Row 2 (WS): K2, P to last 2 sts, K2.
Row 3: K across.
Row 4: Rep Row 2.
Rep Rows 1-4 two more times. 21 sts.
Switch to CC (do not break MC) and work Rows 1-4 once more. 19 sts.

Top
Break CC and switch to MC.
Row 1 (RS): SSK, K to last 2 sts, K2tog. 17 sts.
Row 2 (WS): K2, P to last 2 sts, K2.
Rep Rows 1-2 once more. 15 sts.

Row 5 (RS): SSK, K to last 2 sts, K2tog. 2 sts dec.
Row 6 (WS): SSK, K to last 2 sts, K2tog. 2 sts dec.
Rep Rows 5-6 two more times. 3 sts.

Break yarn and draw through remaining sts.

Finishing
Weave in ends, wash, and block if desired.

Cut a long length of CC. Working from RS, with football's points facing up and down (as opposed to side to side), in between the two white stripes, count up four rows from one of the white stripes. Find the central 3 sts. Duplicate stitch a white stripe on these 3 sts up center of football, stopping four rows from other white stripe.

Cut another length of CC. Create 5-6 "laces," evenly spaced along duplicate stitch stripe, by simply making one very long running stitch approx 1-2 sts wider than the stripe on each side.

Weave in ends from lacing.

FOGGY PATHS
by Stana D. Sortor

This simple, square-shaped dishcloth features a wonderful cable design, reminiscent of a twisty foggy path. Starting with 2x2 Rib, the cable pattern is worked in the middle with Stockinette Stitch panels and a ribbed edge. The dishcloth is finished with another 2x2 Rib pattern border. The last stitch of every row is slipped for a nice edge.

FINISHED MEASUREMENTS
8″ square

YARN
Shine™ (sport weight, 60% Pima Cotton, 40% Modal; 110 yards/50g): Robot 25331, 1 skein

NEEDLES
US 5 (3.75mm) straight or circular needles

NOTIONS
Yarn Needle
Stitch Markers
Cable Needle

GAUGE
28 sts and 32 rows = 4″ in Stockinette Stitch, blocked

4/5 RC-P1 (cable 4 over 5 right, purl 1 back)
Sl5 to CN, hold in back; K4, (K4, P1) from CN.

4/5 LC-P1 (cable 4 over 5 left, purl 1 back)
Sl4 to CN, hold in front; P1, K4, K4 from CN.

4/5 RC-Pc (cable 4 over 5 right, purl center)
Sl5 to CN, hold in back; K4, (P1, K4) from CN.

4/5 LC-Pc (cable 4 over 5 left, purl center)
Sl4 to CN, hold in front; K4, P1, K4 from CN.

5/4 RC-P1 (cable 5 over 4 right, purl 1 front)
Sl4 to CN, hold in back; P1, K4, K4 from CN.

5/4 LC-P1 (cable 5 over 4 left, purl 1 front)
Sl5 to CN, hold in front; K4, (K4, P1) from CN.

4/4 LC (cable 4 over 4 left)
Sl4 to CN, hold in front; K4, K4 from CN.

DIRECTIONS
CO 58 sts. Work from Foggy Paths Cable chart (next page) or follow the written directions below.

Row 1 (RS): (K2, P2) 14 times, K1, Sl1 WYIF.
Row 2 (WS): (P2, K2) 14 times, P1, Sl1 WYIF.
Rows 3–10: Rep Rows 1–2.
Row 11: (K2, P2) two times, K10, P2, K4, P1, K8, P1, K4, P2, K10, P2, K2, P2, K1, Sl1 WYIF.
Row 12: (P2, K2) two times, P10, K2, P4, K1, P8, K1, P4, K2, P10, K2, P2, K2, P1, Sl1 WYIF.
Rows 13–14: Rep Rows 11–12.
Row 15: (K2, P2) two times, K10, P2, 4/5 RC-P1, 4/5 LC-P1, P2, K10, P2, K2, P2, K1, Sl1 WYIF.
Row 16: (P2, K2) two times, P10, K2, P8, K2, P8, K2, P10, K2, P2, K2, P1, Sl1 WYIF.
Row 17: (K2, P2) two times, K10, P2, K8, P2, K8, P2, K10, P2, K2, P2, K1, Sl1 WYIF.
Rows 18–22: Rep Rows 16–17.
Row 23: (K2, P2) two times, K10, P2, 4/5 RC-Pc, 4/5 LC-Pc, P2, K10, P2, K2, P2, K1, Sl1 WYIF.
Rows 24–28: Rep Rows 12 and 11.
Row 29: (K2, P2) two times, K10, P2, K4, P1, 4/4 LC, P1, K4, P2, K10, P2, K2, P2, K1, Sl1 WYIF.
Rows 30–34: Rep Rows 12 and 11.
Row 35: Rep Row 29.
Rows 36–40: Rep Rows 12 and 11.
Row 41: (K2, P2) two times, K10, P2, 5/4 LC-P1, 5/4 RC-P1, P2, K10, P2, K2, P2, K1, Sl1 WYIF.
Rows 42–48: Rep Rows 16–17.
Row 49: (K2, P2) two times, K10, P2, 4/5 LC-Pc, 4/5 RC-Pc, P2, K10, P2, K2, P2, K1, Sl1 WYIF.
Rows 50–54: Rep Rows 12 and 11.
Rows 55–64: Rep Rows 1–2.

BO in 2x2 Rib pattern.

Finishing
Weave in ends, wash, and block to measurements.

Foggy Paths Cable

LEGEND

K
RS: Knit stitch
WS: Purl stitch

P
RS: Purl stitch
WS: Knit stitch

Sl
RS: Slip stitch purl-wise, with yarn in back
WS: Slip stitch purl-wise, with yarn in front

Sl WYIF
RS: Slip stitch purl-wise, with yarn in front
WS: Slip stitch purl-wise, with yarn in back

Cable 4 Over 4 Left (4/4 LC)
Sl4 to CN, hold in front; K4, K4 from CN

Cable 4 Over 5 Right, purl 1 back (4/5 RC-P1)
Sl5 to CN, hold in back; K4, (K4, P1) from CN

Cable 4 Over 5 Left, purl 1 back (4/5 LC-P1)
Sl4 to CN, hold in front; P1, K4, K4 from CN

Cable 4 Over 5 Right, purl center (4/5 RC-Pc)
Sl5 to CN, hold in back; K4, (P1, K4) from CN

Cable 4 Over 5 Left, purl center (4/5 LC-Pc)
Sl4 to CN, hold in front; K4, P1, K4 from CN

Cable 5 Over 4 Right, purl 1 front (5/4 RC-P1)
Sl4 to CN, hold in back; P1, K4, K4 from CN

Cable 5 Over 4 Left, purl 1 front (5/4 LC-P1)
Sl5 to CN, hold in front; K4, (K4, P1) from CN

HERRING
by Violet LeBeaux

Herring is a dishcloth featuring a lifted herringbone stitch diagonally across the cloth. The lifted stitches stack into neat textured columns. The other half of the cloth is Stockinette and it has a slipped stitch edge. The slipped nature of the herringbone breaks up multi-coloured yarns effectively and the stiffness of the stitch makes it great for scrubbing.

FINISHED MEASUREMENTS
7" width × 6.75" height

YARN
Dishie™ (worsted weight, 100% Cotton; 190 yards/100g): Silver 25789, 1 skein

NEEDLES
US 6 (4mm) straight or circular needles

NOTIONS
Yarn Needle

GAUGE
18 sts and 24 rows = 4" in Stockinette Stitch, blocked
18 sts and 24 rows = 4" in lace pattern, blocked

PSBL
Pass slipped stitch over and move it back onto LH needle, knit slipped stitch through the back loop.

P2TP
P2tog but do not drop sts off LH needle. Purl through first st on LH needle then drop both sts from LH needle.

DIRECTIONS
Loosely CO 32 sts.

Row 1 (RS): Sl1, K to end.
Row 2 (WS): Sl1, P to end.
Rows 3-6: Rep Rows 1-2 two more times.

Row 7: Sl1, K2 (Sl1, K1, PSBL) 13 times (or to last 3 sts), K to end.
Row 8: Sl1, P2, (P2TP) to last 3 sts, P3.
Row 9: Sl1, K2 (Sl1, K1, PSBL) twelve times (or to last 5 sts), K to end.
Row 10: Sl1, P4, (P2TP) to last 3 sts, P3.

Row 11: Sl1, K2 (Sl1, K1, PSBL) eleven times (or to last 7 sts), K to end.
Row 12: Sl1, P6, (P2TP) to last 3 sts, P3.
Rep Rows 11-12 ten more times as established, each time working one fewer rep on RS rows and 2 more P sts on WS rows to match.

Rep Rows 1-4.
BO all sts.

Finishing
Weave in ends, wash, and block to measurements.

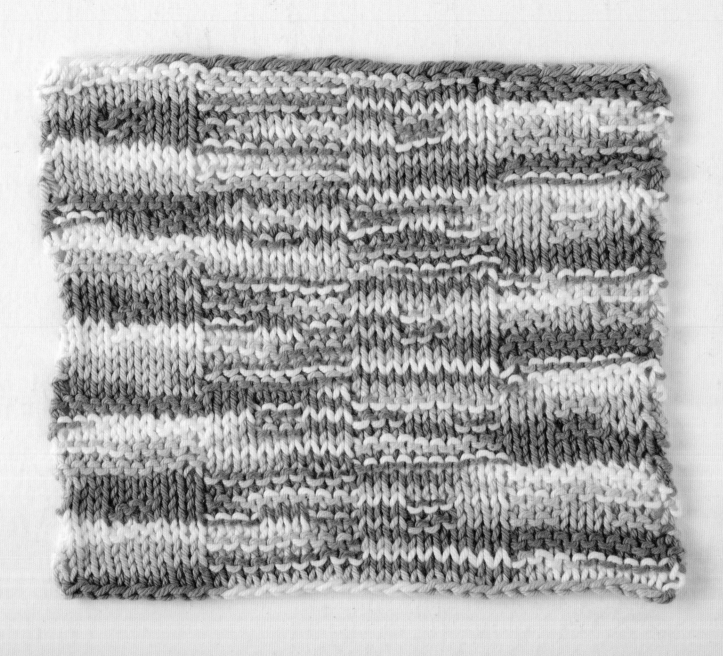

BANDERA
by Joyce Fassbender

Like a creek bed, this dishcloth features a bumpy texture with smooth spots, perfect for scrubbing those dishes! Mixing Stockinette Stitch and Garter Stitch means this is a great project for beginners looking for a new project or expert knitters wanting a quick mindless treat. This is also a perfect project for both solid and multi-colored yarns.

FINISHED MEASUREMENTS
8″ square

YARN
Dishie™ Multi (worsted weight, 100% Cotton; 190 yards/100g): Pebble 27336, 1 skein

NEEDLES
US 7 (4.5mm) straight or circular needles

NOTIONS
Yarn Needle

GAUGE
19 sts and 28 rows = 4″ in Stockinette Stitch, blocked

DIRECTIONS
CO 38 sts using a Long Tail Cast On.
Setup Row: K across.

Row 1: K1, (K9, P9) two times, K1.
Row 2: K1, P to last st, K1.
Row 3: K1, (K9, P9) two times, K1.
Row 4: K1, (P12, K3, P3) two times, K1.
Row 5: K1, (K9, P3, K3, P3) two times, K1.
Row 6: K1, (P12, K3, P3) two times, K1.
Row 7: K1, (K9, P9) two times, K1.
Row 8: K1, P to last st, K1.
Row 9: K1, (K9, P9) two times, K1.
Row 10: K1, (K9, P9) two times, K1.
Row 11: K across.
Row 12: K1, (P9, K9) two times, K1.
Row 13: K1, (K12, P3, K3) two times, K1.
Row 14: K1, (P9, K3, P3, K3) two times, K1.
Row 15: K1, (K12, P3, K3) two times, K1.
Row 16: K1, (P9, K9) two times, K1.
Row 17: K across.
Row 18: K1, (P9, K9) two times, K1.
Rep Rows 1–18.
Rep Rows 1–9 once more.

Ending Row: P across.
BO all sts.

Finishing
Weave in ends, wash, and block.

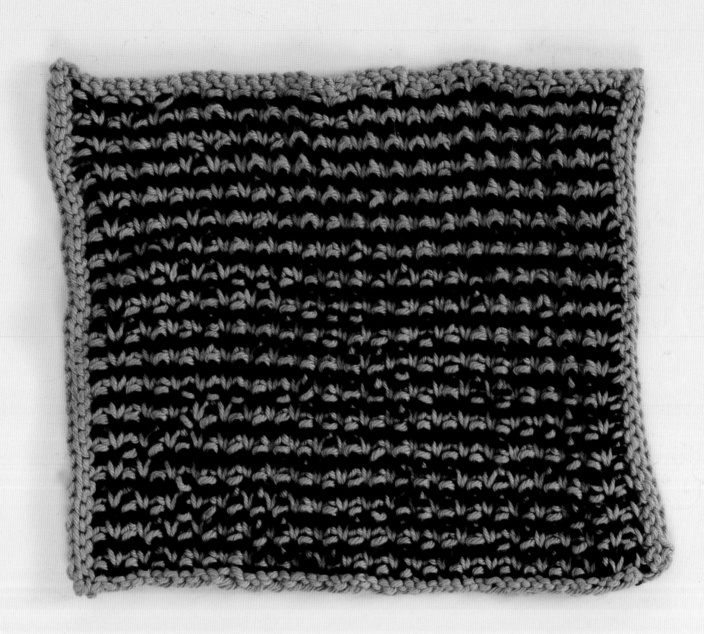

TEXTURAMA!
by Ann Weaver

Need a dishcloth with some heavy duty scrubbing power that is also fun to knit? Texturama! is for you! Using two contrasting colors, the fun texture is created with simple slipped stitches, creating a surface that is perfect for washing those dishes.

Texturama! is knit in one piece, using one color per row. Carry unused color up the sides for fewer ends to weave in. The edging is knit along the edges of the dishcloth to prevent the edges from curling in.

FINISHED MEASUREMENTS
8" × 7"

YARN
Dishie™ (worsted weight, 100% Cotton; 190 yards/100g): MC Silver 25789, CC Black 26669, 1 skein each

NEEDLES
US 7 (4.5mm) straight or circular needles

NOTIONS
Yarn Needle

GAUGE
20 sts and 40 rows = 4" in Garter Stitch, blocked

DIRECTIONS
Using a Long Tail Cast On and MC, CO 45 sts.
Join CC, but do not break MC.

Begin working Texture Pattern as follows.
Row 1 (RS): Using CC, (K1, Sl1 WYIB) to last st, K1.
Row 2 (WS): Using CC, (K1, bring yarn to front of work, Sl1 WYIF, bring yarn to back of work) to last st, K1.
Rows 3–4: Using MC, rep Rows 1–2.

Rep Rows 1–4 17 times (18 total reps of 4-row Texture Pattern).
Work Rows 1–2 once more.

Break CC.
BO loosely using MC.

Edging
Using MC, with RS facing, PU and K 35 sts evenly spaced along right edge of dishcloth.
Knit one row.
BO loosely.

Rep all Edging steps for left edge of dishcloth.

Finishing
Weave in ends, wash, and enjoy!

ARACHNOPHOBIA
by Lee Meredith

Make a creepy knitted spiderweb for Halloween season cleanup! Use classic black and white, or do your own thing for a colorful cobweb in any two contrasting colors. The web strands are made by slipping the web yarn loosely across long sections of stitches, and then twisting the strands around knit stitches on later rounds.

FINISHED MEASUREMENTS
11" across

YARN
CotLin™ (DK weight, 70% Tanguis Cotton, 30% Linen; 123 yards/50g): MC Black 24468, CC Swan 24134, 1 skein each

NEEDLES
US 6 (4 mm) DPNs or 40" or longer circular needles for Magic Loop method

NOTIONS
Yarn Needle
Stitch Marker
Blocking Pins

GAUGE
18 sts and 28 rows = 4" in Stockinette Stitch in the round, blocked (stretched out significantly to block)

Pattern Notes
Keep the contrasting color yarn very loose across the long groups of slipped stitches by stretching the stitches out across the needle to prevent the yarn from pulling in—if you have a hard time, you can choose to wrap the yarn around the needle twice when working the decrease stitch, then drop the extra wrap off the needle when slipping that stitch on the following round.

The chart is worked in the round; read each chart row from right to left as a RS row. Note: the first two rounds are technically worked flat, across the RS, because the piece has not yet been joined in the round.

The first few rows of the chart are written out in detail to help get you started. After working those, you'll be able to read your knitting to see which stitches to slip (always slipping CC sts on MC rows) and when to work decreases, based on the yarn colors.

DIRECTIONS
CO 132 sts with MC, leaving a tail at least 8" long. Begin working flat, starting with a WS row; cont flat until joining in the rnd at the beginning of chart Rnd 3.
Setup Rows 1–3 (MC): K across.

Work from chart (next page), repeating chart sts three times across.

On Row 1 and all CC rnds through Rnd 37, bring yarn to front to slip sts, then bring yarn through to back to work dec.

First Three Chart Rows
Row 1 (RS) (CC): Sl15 WYIF, bring yarn to back (right now it's just a long, loose tail, make sure it's at least 12" long—you'll be using this tail later, as the first spiderweb strand), CDD, bring yarn to front, Sl23, bring yarn to back, stretch out the 23 slipped sts to loosen CC yarn across them, CDD, *bring yarn to front and Sl15, bring yarn to back, stretch out the 15 slipped sts to loosen CC yarn across them, CCD, (cont bringing yarn to front and back and loosening across in the same way) Sl23 WYIF, CDD; rep from * once more.
Slide sts across needle(s) to begin next row on other side (where MC yarn is hanging) and work flat across RS.
Row 2 (RS) (MC): (K15, Sl1 WYIF, K23, Sl1 WYIB) three times (slipping the CC sts).
Rnd 3 (RS) (MC): Join to work in the rnd and PM for BOR; rep Row 2.
When beginning Rnd 4, bring CC yarn tail across RS to BOR and wrap it once around the MC yarn running across, to hold it in place across the first set of MC sts.

On Rnd 5 and all following CC rnds with CDDs, the CDD will go across BOR and include first st of next rnd; remove and replace BOR M to stay immediately after CDD st.

Cont working chart to end, break yarn, thread through remaining 6 sts and draw tight to close hole.

Finishing
Use CO tail to sew up the gap between the first few rows that were worked flat.

Weave in ends, wash, and block by pinning down. Stretch hard by pulling across each of the points with your hands, then pin down each of the six points and let dry completely.

Spiderweb Chart

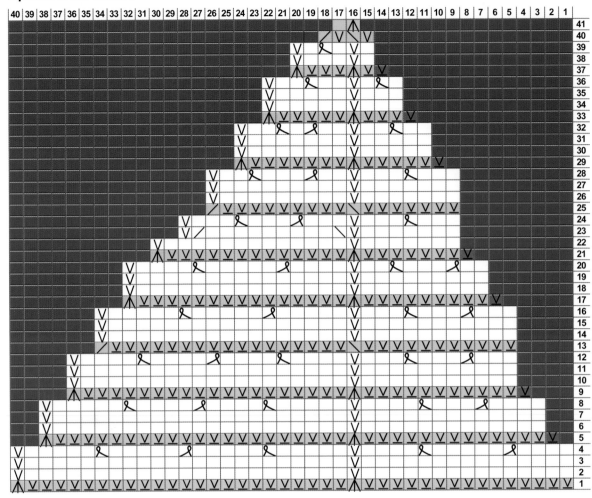

LEGEND

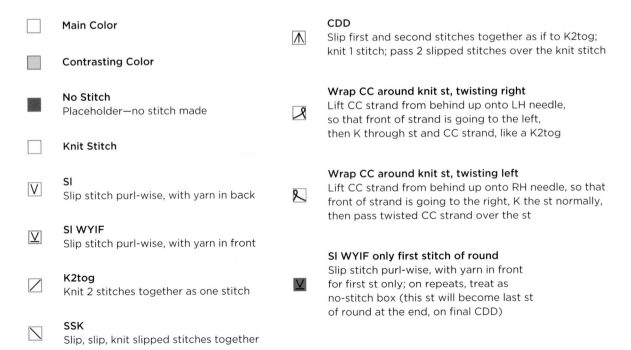

	Main Color
	Contrasting Color
	No Stitch — Placeholder—no stitch made
	Knit Stitch
V	**Sl** — Slip stitch purl-wise, with yarn in back
V	**Sl WYIF** — Slip stitch purl-wise, with yarn in front
/	**K2tog** — Knit 2 stitches together as one stitch
\	**SSK** — Slip, slip, knit slipped stitches together

CDD
Slip first and second stitches together as if to K2tog; knit 1 stitch; pass 2 slipped stitches over the knit stitch

Wrap CC around knit st, twisting right
Lift CC strand from behind up onto LH needle, so that front of strand is going to the left, then K through st and CC strand, like a K2tog

Wrap CC around knit st, twisting left
Lift CC strand from behind up onto RH needle, so that front of strand is going to the right, K the st normally, then pass twisted CC strand over the st

Sl WYIF only first stitch of round
Slip stitch purl-wise, with yarn in front for first st only; on repeats, treat as no-stitch box (this st will become last st of round at the end, on final CDD)

Glossary

Common Stitches & Techniques

Slipped Stitches (Sl)
Always slip stitches purl-wise with yarn held to the wrong side of work, unless noted otherwise in the pattern.

Make 1 Left-Leaning Stitch (M1L)
Inserting LH needle from front to back, PU the horizontal strand between the st just worked and the next st, and K TBL.

Make 1 Right-Leaning Stitch (M1R)
Inserting LH needle from back to front, PU the horizontal strand between the st just worked and the next st, and K TFL.

Slip, Slip, Knit (SSK)
(Sl1 K-wise) twice; insert LH needle into front of these 2 sts and knit them together.

Centered Double Decrease (CDD)
Slip first and second sts together as if to work K2tog; K1; pass 2 slipped sts over the knit st.

Stockinette Stitch (St st, flat over any number of sts)
Row 1 (RS): Knit all sts.
Row 2 (WS): Purl all sts.
Rep Rows 1-2 for pattern.
St st in the round: Knit every rnd.

Garter Stitch (in the round over any number of sts)
Rnd 1: Purl all sts.
Rnd 2: Knit all sts.
Rep Rnds 1-2 for pattern.
Garter Stitch flat: Knit every row.
(One Garter ridge is comprised of two rows/rnds.)

1x1 Rib (flat or in the round, over an even number of sts)
Row/Rnd 1: (K1, P1) to end of row/rnd.
Rep Row/Rnd 1 for pattern.

2x2 Rib (flat over a multiple of 4 sts plus 2)
Row 1 (RS): K2, (P2, K2) to end of row.
Row 2 (WS): P2, (K2, P2) to end of row.
Rep Rows 1-2 for pattern.

2x2 Rib (in the round over a multiple of 4 sts)
Rnd 1: (K2, P2) to end of rnd.
Rep Rnd 1 for pattern.

Magic Loop Technique
A technique using one long circular needle to knit in the round around a small circumference. A tutorial can be found at https://tutorials.knitpicks.com/wptutorials/magic-loop.

Knitting in the Round with Two Circular Needles
A technique using two long circulars to knit around a small circumference. A tutorial can be found at https://tutorials.knitpicks.com/knitting-in-the-round-with-2-circular-needles.

Backward Loop Cast On
A simple, all-purpose cast on that can be worked mid-row. Also called Loop, Single, or E-Wrap Cast On. A tutorial can be found at https://tutorials.knitpicks.com/loop-cast-on.

Long Tail Cast On
Fast and neat once you get the hang of it. Also referred to as the Slingshot Cast On. A tutorial can be found at https://tutorials.knitpicks.com/long-tail-cast-on.

Cabled Cast On
A strong and nice looking basic cast on that can be worked mid-project. A tutorial can be found at https://tutorials.knitpicks.com/cabled-cast-on.

3-Needle Bind Off
Used to easily seam two rows of live stitches together. A tutorial can be found at https://tutorials.knitpicks.com/3-needle-bind-off.

Abbreviations

approx	approximately	KFB	knit into front and back of stitch	PSSO	pass slipped stitch over	SSP	slip, slip, purl these 2 stitches together through back loop
BO	bind off			PU	pick up		
BOR	beginning of round	K-wise	knit-wise	P-wise	purl-wise	SSSK	slip, slip, slip, knit these 3 stitches together (like SSK)
CN	cable needle	LH	left hand	rep	repeat		
C (1, 2...)	color (1, 2...)	M	marker	Rev St st	reverse stockinette stitch		
CC	contrast color	M1	make 1 stitch			St st	stockinette stitch (*see above*)
CDD	centered double decrease (*see above*)	M1L	make 1 left-leaning stitch (*see above*)	RH	right hand	st(s)	stitch(es)
		M1R	make 1 right-leaning stitch (*see above*)	rnd(s)	round(s)	TBL	through back loop
CO	cast on			RS	right side	TFL	through front loop
cont	continue	MC	main color	Sk	skip	tog	together
dec(s)	decrease(es)	P	purl	SK2P	slip 1, knit 2 together, pass slipped stitch over	W&T	wrap & turn (for short rows; *see next pg*)
DPN(s)	double pointed needle(s)	P2tog	purl 2 stitches together				
inc(s)	increase(s)	P3tog	purl 3 stitches together	SKP	slip, knit, pass slipped stitch over	WE	work even
K	knit			SI	slip (*see above*)	WS	wrong side
K2tog	knit 2 stitches together	PM	place marker	SM	slip marker	WYIB	with yarn in back
		PFB	purl into front and back of stitch	SSK	slip, slip, knit these 2 stitches together (*see above*)	WYIF	with yarn in front
K3tog	knit 3 stitches together					YO	yarn over

Cabling Without a Cable Needle

Tutorials for 1 over 1 cables can be found at https://blog.knitpicks.com/tutorial-1-over-1-cables-without-a-cable-needle. A tutorial for standard cables can be found at https://tutorials.knitpicks.com/learn-to-cable-without-a-cable-needle.

Felted Join (to splice yarn)

One method for joining a new length of yarn to the end of one that is already being used. A tutorial can be found at https://tutorials.knitpicks.com/felted-join.

Mattress Stitch

A neat, invisible seaming method that uses the bars between the first and second stitches on the edges. A tutorial can be found at https://tutorials.knitpicks.com/mattress-stitch.

Provisional Cast On (crochet method)

Used to cast on stitches that are also a row of live stitches, so they can be put onto a needle and used later.

Directions: Using a crochet hook, make a slipknot, then hold knitting needle in left hand, hook in right. With yarn in back of needle, work a chain st by pulling yarn over needle and through chain st. Move yarn back to behind needle, and rep for the number of sts required. Chain a few more sts off the needle, then break yarn and pull end through last chain. (CO sts may be incorrectly mounted; if so, work into backs of these sts.) To unravel later (when sts need to be picked up), pull chain end out; chain should unravel, leaving live sts. A video tutorial can be found at https://tutorials.knitpicks.com/crocheted-provisional-cast-on.

Provisional Cast On (crochet chain method)

Same result as the crochet method above, but worked differently, so you may prefer one or the other.

Directions: With a crochet hook, use scrap yarn to make a slipknot and chain the number of sts to be cast on, plus a few extra sts. Insert tip of knitting needle into first bump of crochet chain. Wrap project yarn around needle as if to knit, and pull yarn through crochet chain, forming first st. Rep this process until you have cast on the correct number of sts. To unravel later (when sts need to be picked up), pull chain out, leaving live sts. A photo tutorial can be found at https://tutorials.knitpicks.com/crocheted-provisional-cast-on.

Judy's Magic Cast On

This method creates stitches coming out in opposite directions from a seamless center line, perfect for starting toe-up socks.

Directions: Make a slipknot and place loop around one of the two needles; anchor loop counts as first st. Hold needles tog, with needle that yarn is attached to on top. In other hand, hold yarn so tail goes over index finger and yarn attached to ball goes over thumb. Bring tip of bottom needle over strand of yarn on finger (top strand), around and under yarn and back up, making a loop around needle. Pull loop snug. Bring top needle (with slipknot) over yarn tail on thumb (bottom strand), around and under yarn and back up, making a loop around needle. Pull loop snug. Cont casting on sts until desired number is reached; top yarn strand always wraps around bottom needle, and bottom yarn strand always wraps around top needle. A tutorial can be found at https://tutorials.knitpicks.com/judys-magic-cast-on.

Stretchy Bind Off

Directions: K2, *insert LH needle into front of 2 sts on RH needle and knit them tog—1 st remains on RH needle. K1; rep from * until all sts have been bound off. A tutorial can be found at https://tutorials.knitpicks.com/go-your-own-way-socks-toe-up-part-7-binding-off.

Jeny's Surprisingly Stretchy Bind Off (for 1x1 Rib)

Directions: Reverse YO, K1, pass YO over; *YO, P1, pass YO and previous st over P1; reverse YO, K1, pass YO and previous st over K1; rep from * until 1 st is left, then break working yarn and pull it through final st to complete BO.

Kitchener Stitch (also called Grafting)

Seamlessly join two sets of live stitches together.

Directions: With an equal number of sts on two needles, break yarn leaving a tail approx four times as long as the row of sts, and thread through a blunt yarn needle. Hold needles parallel with WSs facing in and both needles pointing to the right. Perform Step 2 on the first front st, then Step 4 on the first back st, then continue from Step 1, always pulling yarn tightly so the grafted row tension matches the knitted fabric:

Step 1: Pull yarn needle K-wise through front st and drop st from knitting needle.

Step 2: Pull yarn needle P-wise through next front st, leaving st on knitting needle.

Step 3: Pull yarn needle P-wise through first back st and drop st from knitting needle.

Step 4: Pull yarn needle K-wise through next back st, leaving st on knitting needle.

Rep Steps 1-4 until all sts have been grafted together, finishing by working Step 1 through the last remaining front st, then Step 3 through the last remaining back st. Photo tutorials can be found at https://blog.knitpicks.com/tutorial-grafting-with-kitchener-stitch-stockinette-garter.

Short Rows

There are several options for how to handle short rows, so you may see different suggestions/intructions in a pattern.

Wrap and Turn (W&T) (one option for Short Rows)

Work until the st to be wrapped. If knitting: Bring yarn to front, Sl next st P-wise, return yarn to back; turn work, and Sl wrapped st onto RH needle. Cont across row. If purling: Bring yarn to back of work, Sl next st P-wise, return yarn to front; turn work and Sl wrapped st onto RH needle. Cont across row.

Picking up Wraps: Work to wrapped st. If knitting: Insert RH needle under wrap, then through wrapped st K-wise; K st and wrap tog. If purling: Sl wrapped st P-wise onto RH needle, use LH needle to lift wrap and place it onto RH needle; Sl wrap and st back onto LH needle, and P tog.

A tutorial for W&T can be found at https://tutorials.knitpicks.com/short-rows-wrap-and-turn-or-wt.

German Short Rows (another option for Short Rows)

Work to turning point; turn. WYIF, Sl first st P-wise. Bring yarn over back of right needle, pulling firmly to create a "double stitch" on RH needle. If next st is a K st, leave yarn at back; if next st is a P st, bring yarn to front between needles. When it's time to work into double st, knit both strands tog.

MEET THE DESIGNERS

Joyce Fassbender has been designing knitted accessories and home goods since 2009. Joyce teaches biology in sunny south Florida, but when she's not at work, she's obsessing over shawls and lace. She also enjoys playing with her dog Polly, looking at bugs, kayaking, and beach combing, but always has her knitting with her, just in case. *For pattern support, please contact joycef2@gmail.com.*

Faith Schmidt designs under the name DistractedKnits for a very good reason. With nine children in the house, there's always something going on! This has led her to design patterns that are interesting to knit, but are also easy to memorize and "read", in case of one of those all-too-frequent interruptions. Faith can be found online at DistractedKnits.weebly.com and on Ravelry, Pinterest, Instagram, and Twitter as DistractedKnits. *For pattern support, please contact distractedknits@hotmail.com.*

Allison Griffith is a lifelong knitter with years of experience designing patterns and teaching fiber arts. She is the creator and author of the blog On the Needles (ontheneedles.com) where she offers patterns, tutorials, and inspiration to hundreds of readers. When not knitting, Allison divides her time between working in her garden, watching too many *Law & Order* reruns, and playing with her dog. *For pattern support, please contact knittingontheneedles@gmail.com.*

Stana D. Sortor's grandmother taught her how to knit and crochet when she was a little girl. Ever since she learned to knit and crochet she took her projects everywhere. Of course she has experienced some sidesteps on her knitting path, like trying to be an artist, photographer, or writer, but she always returned to her favorite activity. Find Stana on her blog Stana's Critters Etc and on Ravelry as Fifinka. *For pattern support, please contact crowsd@yahoo.com.*

Violet LeBeaux loves strong tea, knitting, watercolors, spinning, stickers, and writing lists. A knitwear blogger for close to 10 years, Violet and her easy-to-follow craft patterns, videos, and tutorials have been viewed by millions of people around the world at violetlebeaux.com. *For pattern support, please contact violetlebeaux@gmail.com.*

A former Assyriologist and state bureaucrat, **Ann Weaver** currently works as a bread baker. Her designs, inspired by her friends, family, and her own proto-punk aesthetic, can be found in print and internet publications like Interweave Knits and knitty.com. Her favorite things include dark beers, napping, cycling, and reading a wide variety of literature. *For pattern support, please contact weaverknits77@gmail.com.*

Emily Ringelman lives in Baton Rouge, Louisiana, a place known more for alligators and gumbo than its knitting designers, but hey, a passion is a passion. Find her on Ravelry as EmilyRingelman. *For pattern support, please contact emily.ringelman@gmail.com.*

Knitting is a form of meditation for some people and **Jenny Williams** is happy to be among them. She loves the whole process: perusing stitch dictionaries, sketching, swatching, knitting … even blocking! And when it all comes together, nothing is better. *For pattern support, please contact jennyw@tcworks.net.*

THIS COLLECTION FEATURES

Dishie™
Worsted Weight
100% Cotton

Dishie™ Multi
Worsted Weight
100% Cotton

Dishie™ Twist
Worsted Weight
100% Cotton

CotLin™
DK Weight
70% Tanguis Cotton, 30% Linen

Shine™
Sport Weight
60% Pima Cotton, 40% Modal'

View these beautiful
yarns and more at
www.KnitPicks.com

Knit Picks yarn is both luxe and affordable—a seeming contradiction
trounced! But it's not just about the pretty colors; we also care
deeply about fiber quality and fair labor practices, leaving you with
a gorgeously reliable product you'll turn to time and time again.